D0463630

"*Match in the Root Cellar* is a must read for any senior leader facing an organizational performance crisis. The book identifies the root cause of most dysfunctional organizations and clearly articulates steps that can be taken to eliminate or significantly reduce the problem."

CRAIG BAMBROUGH

Major General, US Army (Retired)

"Chris McGoff opens a window on solutions to workplace problems that invariably nag, undermine, and vex real leaders. Chris writes with the confidence and pen of a novelist, making *Match in the Root Cellar* delightfully readable while offering the hard-headed, practical guidance of a reformer. I would commend this book to anyone who is serious about improving their organization's culture."

ROBERT B. CHARLES

former US Assistant Secretary of State, policy maker, litigator, reformer, and author

"Cultivating a high-performance culture is a challenge for any business leader. In *Match in the Root Cellar*, Chris McGoff illustrates the transformative power of peak performance culture and provides invaluable and actionable insight for how to get there."

TED HALSTEAD

CEO of Climate Leadership Council, author, and public speaker

MATCH IN THE ROOT CELLAR

Strike your match!

[signature]

MATCH IN THE ROOT CELLAR

HOW YOU CAN **SPARK** A
PEAK PERFORMANCE CULTURE

CHRIS McGOFF

AUTHOR OF *THE PRIMES*

ILLUSTRATED BY **JIM NUTTLE**

ForbesBooks

Published by ForbesBooks, Charleston, South Carolina.
Member of Advantage Media Group.

ForbesBooks is a registered trademark, and the ForbesBooks colophon is a trademark of Forbes Media, LLC.

Printed in the United States of America.

10 9 8 7 6 5 4 3 2 1

ISBN: 978-1-94663-312-5
LCCN: 2017946369

Cover design and layout by George Stevens.
Illustrations by Jim Nuttle.

This publication is designed to provide accurate and authoritative information in regard to the subject matter covered. It is sold with the understanding that the publisher is not engaged in rendering legal, accounting, or other professional services. If legal advice or other expert assistance is required, the services of a competent professional person should be sought.

ForbesBooks is proud to be a part of the Tree Neutral® program. Tree Neutral offsets the number of trees consumed in the production and printing of this book by taking proactive steps such as planting trees in direct proportion to the number of trees used to print books. To learn more about Tree Neutral, please visit **www.treeneutral.com**.

Since 1917, the Forbes mission has remained constant. Global Champions of Entrepreneurial Capitalism. ForbesBooks exists to further that aim by bringing the Stories, Passion, and Knowledge of top thought leaders to the forefront. ForbesBooks brings you The Best in Business. To be considered for publication, please visit **www.forbesbooks.com**.

To those of you who freely choose to stand on the front lines of possibility. You know the dangers of taking on the status quo, but you are driven by principle. And you are willing to endure in your stand for as long as it takes. You are not satisfied sitting in the stands and observing the world, content to inherit the future. You live to get on the court and create the future. You are the morally courageous, and our world needs you now more than ever.

To the children of the world. You deserve good ancestors.

ACKNOWLEDGMENTS

The men and women of The Clearing—Your courage is infectious. You take on the biggest systems in the world, participate in the most senior conversations on the planet, and win and lose in the game of whole-system transformation. You persist. There is no knowledge in the absence of experience, and you are the fount of experience that generates the knowledge of this book.

John Miller—We have been business partners for twenty-five years now. Know that you had as much to do with this book being what it is and getting completed as anyone. You are an even hand in a chaotic world.

Kristin Hackler—I had an idea for how to approach this book. Then I met you. You introduced me to Carolyn, Raj, Batya, and the rest of the gang at Phossium. Kristin, your imprint on this book is significant. I went into this project thinking of you as my ghostwriter. I soon realized you were my writing partner. I enjoyed every minute of our collaboration.

Advantage | ForbesBooks—You folks are the velvet hammer. You brought the critical cocktail of creativity with deadlines to our party.

Jim Nuttle—From your commitment to chiseling The PRIMES down to their eternal essence, to your frontline visualization of senior conversations, to your artwork throughout this book, you have the gift of making visions visible. Jim, you are a gifted illustrator. You "show" us what we need to see.

My six adult children and all the friends you brought into my world—You let me into your world and allowed me to make your friends my friends. You helped me see the brilliance of young leaders coming into their own. You blew apart the myths and stereotypes of Generation X and Millennials and showed me how, regardless of age, we really are pretty much the same. You gave me the gift of listening and encouraged me to write down what has become clear to me. You told me you valued this work. It made all the difference in the world, and in your hands, I know the world is in a good place.

Dr. Rushworth Kidder—Rush, I know you can hear me even though you have left this earth. Your lifetime dedication to helping the world access moral courage and helping good people make tough choices became a source of inspiration. I hope I can make a fraction of the contribution you made in helping people do the right things, right.

ABOUT THE AUTHOR, CHRIS McGOFF

Chris McGoff is a business builder, best-selling author, investor, and advisor to business leaders throughout the world.

He has founded, partnered, and invested in several companies in industries ranging from service and product companies to real estate and cloud-based solution providers. He sits on boards and participates in venture funding to emerging companies. Over the past thirty-five years, Chris has helped hundreds of organizations and tens of thousands of people thrive in the chaos of the modern business environment. Chris likes to say, "If you do something long enough, you eventually figure it out." And he has.

From Silicon Valley to Wall Street, from high-tech start-ups to huge government bureaucracies, from the Miracle Mile in Chicago to the war-torn streets of Afghanistan, people not only find success in applying Chris's advice, but they also find significance and personal fulfillment along the way. Chris's quick wit, charisma, and ability to challenge the status quo and deliver actionable advice based on years of experience have made him a sought-after advisor and public speaker.

What makes Chris McGoff unique is how accessible his advice is. Chris offers understandable, actionable, and time-tested truths about leadership, organizational culture, and getting complicated things accomplished. Chris McGoff is the author of *The PRIMES: How Any Group Can Solve Any Problem*, which has become a desk reference for peak performance leaders.

Chris McGoff is committed to making sure those of us willing to dare noble and mighty things are outfitted with everything we need to be successful. To that end, Chris founded The Clearing, Inc., a management consulting firm located in Washington, DC. The Clearing provides consulting, advising, and training services for leaders committed to driving change and causing transformative outcomes for their organizations.

Chris McGoff is an avid adventure traveler and outdoor enthusiast. He and his wife Claire live in the Washington, DC, area among their six adult children and extended family.

ABOUT THE ILLUSTRATOR, JIM NUTTLE

Jim Nuttle has spent a lifetime drawing pictures. Throughout his career, he has worked with a wide variety of clients in the corporate, nonprofit, and government arenas, and his illustrations have appeared in major publications. His drive has always been to create compelling visuals that inform, engage, and—occasionally—amuse the viewer.

Since 2006, his focus has shifted from the studio to working with groups in live sessions to capture their thoughts in pictures and help them chart their paths going forward. It was through this work that Jim had the good fortune to meet Chris and, since then, to work alongside him with clients across the country—an experience that continues to have a profound impact on his life and career.

Jim lives in Maryland with his wife Nancy, where they marvel at having raised three vibrant, creative individuals.

TABLE OF CONTENTS

INTRODUCTION:
TWO BOOKS, ONE GOAL

The ultimate goal of this book is to help you understand and believe three things:

1) Culture is not some abstract, nebulous, complicated topic; it is as real as steel, and when it's intentionally shaped, you get a tangible result. It is also something you can do—you can shape your culture, and you can do so immediately in a way that others will see and be affected by it. And we're going to show you how in this book.

2) Culture is something you have to generate every day. Like health and love, culture is not a state you achieve and then it automatically stays there—it's something you have to generate intentionally and actively. And when you stop intentionally generating a culture, a default culture is created. So, while you always have culture, you must intentionally generate the culture you *want*, or you will be left with the culture that the world generates for you. This is when you ask yourself whether you want to just get by with a default culture, or do you actively want to be the cause of a great

culture—one in which you and everyone around you are driven to work at their peak performance?

3) There is nothing new in this book. There are things in your life and in your experience that we're going to touch on, and, as you read this, they'll make sense to you. You will recognize that you've been here before, and you'll know it's right. In the end, this book is meant to activate you and, in turn, those around you, until you're all intentionally generating a peak performance culture.

How you are perceived in this world is not in the way you think; it's how you act and what you say. By actively generating a peak performance culture, you create an environment where everything just seems to click. Big things suddenly seem easy to do, and things go fast. You can be intentional about causing these times, and you can do that starting today, on your own.

This belief is one that I've come to understand over the past three decades of working in both large and small groups. From dealing with death calls in my father's small funeral home in Scranton to working for IBM, Frito-Lay, building my own three companies, and being the father of six children, I've been unavoidably immersed in working with groups my entire life. Through this, I've come to understand the simple reality of culture: It is as old as fire, as pervasive as wind, and as inescapable as gravity. It's a part of the human experience, and it will always be around you. But it's on *you* to recognize the culture you have, to know the culture you want, and to actively generate the culture that drives you and everyone else around you to work at peak performance.

CAROLYN'S STORY & STRIKE A MATCH

There are two very clear, very different parts to this book. The first is the story of Carolyn, the newly hired CEO of a firm in need of a culture change, which I call "Carolyn's Story." The second part, "Strike a Match," is more instructional and is meant to serve as a quick reference guide as you work to establish a peak performance culture in your own environment, whatever that may be.

The characters you're about to meet in Carolyn's story are not fiction; they're composites of people you may already be familiar with—individuals who occur in just about every office environment, from the laggards (who may seem to support new ideas in the beginning but turn out to be nothing more than self-appointed guardians of the status quo) to the true supporters, generators, and champions. You work with these people every day, meet them constantly in life, and in reading this book, you'll learn how to recognize them on deeper and more meaningful levels so that when it comes time to instigate change, you will know which ones are able to change, which ones will offer their unwavering support, and which ones you simply need to acknowledge—and then ignore entirely.

Conversely, "Strike a Match" is designed to read as instructionally straightforward as a wilderness survival field guide. This is the section that you can take with you when you decide to strike your own match and ignite a peak performance culture within your own organization. It is your collected journal of knowledge from those who have gone before you, so when you find yourself with a question of culture in your workplace, this guide will quickly and effectively provide you with answers.

The book takes two distinctively different angles, because we understand that the world is full of different learning styles. If you prefer a just-the-facts approach, you're welcome to jump to the back of this book and start briefing yourself on the guide. If you prefer the journey and learn by experience, then the story of Carolyn was written for you.

Regardless of which path you take, I am honored that you're investing your time and this part of your life to learning about what you can do, right now, to change the tide of culture in your workplace. You can change the experience. It's within your power to do it, and when you strike that match to spark a peak performance culture, this book will be here to support you every step of the way.

—Chris McGoff

PART I

CAROLYN'S STORY

CHAPTER 1

MEET CAROLYN QUALEY

arolyn woke up with a start. The sky outside her window was barely hinting at dawn, dark pewter against the black of the trees, but she was wide awake.

Actually, she'd barely been able to fall asleep last night. For days, she'd only been able to think about this moment and what was ahead of her. Today, in a few hours, she would walk into her new job at Phossium Enterprises for the first time as a Chief Executive Officer (CEO).

The house was quiet during her morning routine, the only sound coming from the talking heads on television as they bantered their way through the news. In her small walk-in closet, she quickly stepped into a pencil skirt and blouse that she'd set out the night before, completing the look with a gauzy scarf the color of spring leaves, which set off her hazel eyes. It never took her long to get ready—a lifetime of getting up early to get the kids ready for school, get her husband out the door, and, in the odd remaining seconds, get *herself* ready for work had trained her to whip through her morning routine with almost militaristic efficiency.

She glanced down at the bathroom counter as she ran a brush through her silver-streaked, honey-brown hair, letting it fall naturally into shoulder-length curls. Two antique sterling frames held pictures of her eldest son—a recent graduate from George Washington University with a degree in pre-medicine and currently volunteering with Doctors Without Borders—and her daughter, who was majoring in business administration and Spanish at the University of Virginia. She'd spoken with both of them about her new job, and both were very happy for her.

"You so deserve this, Mom," her daughter had said. "You were practically running that last company on your own, anyway. Now it's just official!"

She'd laughed, both at the comment and the fact that deep down, she'd been thinking the same thing.

Her husband had been congratulatory, too, but only briefly. He was out of the country, and their phone connection was spotty at best, but she knew they'd talk more when he got home next month. At sixty-two years old, he kept swearing he was going to retire from the architectural world soon, but she knew how passionate he was about his job. He'd be on the road for a few more years at least, and she was fine with that. She obviously wasn't ready to stop anytime soon, either.

The hot-orange clouds on the horizon were condensing into a brilliant sunrise as she slid into the car to leave. But before she switched on the engine, she sat for just a moment, closed her eyes, and took a deep breath. This was the moment she'd waited for her whole life, and she was ready for it. Everything she'd done throughout her career had built to this, and today was the day that everything changed: for her career, for herself—and for the company. She was ready to dedicate herself completely to turning her new organization into something spectacular, something she could be proud of and that would carry her mark on it for decades to come. Her focus, from this day on, was the transformation of Phossium Enterprises into an industry leader that clients and team members alike would boast about being a part of.

SHE WAS READY TO DEDICATE HERSELF COMPLETELY TO

TURNING HER NEW ORGANIZATION INTO SOMETHING SPECTACULAR.

With one more deep breath, she exhaled, smiled, turned on the car, and took off down the road.

CHAPTER 2

MEETING WITH THE BOARD

As much as she wanted to walk in the front door of Phossium and hit the ground running, Carolyn had to take care of her corporate obligations first, which meant that before she could settle into her new office, she first had to attend a "welcome-aboard" meeting with the company owners.

She'd met with several company reps during her interview process and even knew some of them from her previous job. It was this group, Algus Consolidated Systems, that had purchased her old company while she was still serving there as interim director. In fact, it was her sharp business acumen and success with the acquisition process that had encouraged Algus's board of directors to consider her for the CEO position at Phossium— another company that they'd only recently acquired.

Today, as she officially stepped into her new role, she would also meet with the entire board to ensure they were all on the same page in regard to what they wanted to see happen with this new acquisition. Phossium was going to play an integral role in Algus's infrastructure, but only if it could prove to be both productive and profitable—two factors that she understood were already shaky for the thirty-year-old company.

The boardroom was on the fourth floor, but she took the stairs, enjoying the brief burst of physical effort. It was all she could do not to jog up each flight, but there would be time for a run when she got home. Plus, that energy needed to go into making a solid, positive impression with her new bosses . . . and it wouldn't help if that first impression was of her in a sheen of sweat.

Even though Carolyn was early, several people were already there to greet her as she walked in. She said hello, shook hands, and chatted for a minute before taking her seat. Right at 8:00 a.m., the meeting began.

At first there were no real surprises; the board reinforced exactly what they'd told her during her interviews: Phossium had once been a decent company but had been in a slow decline for years. It was her job to identify the problems, clean them up, and transition the company into a functioning and profitable member of the Algus family.

Carolyn already had several ideas on where to start, but just as Bertrand Wagner, the director of the board, opened the floor to her, the door flung open.

"Gentlemen, ladies, good morning, my apologies," said a tall, elegant woman as she strode in, a large, expensive-looking purse carefully nested in the crook of her bare arm. She gave the room a deep, heartfelt smile before settling gracefully into an empty chair, drawing a black leather-bound tablet out of her bag and flicking it on. After a moment, she looked up in surprise as though startled at the silence.

"Well, don't let me interrupt, Bert," she said to the director, who flinched ever so slightly at the nickname. "What's on the table?"

"Good morning, Dolores," the director replied with a hard-but-polite smile. "I had just handed the floor over to our new CEO, Mrs. Carolyn Qualey, when you walked in."

"Mrs. Qualey," the director continued, "this is Dolores Pendergrast. She's the most recent member elected to our board and whom you'll be reporting to from here on out. I'm sure you'll have a lot to talk about after this meeting, but first, you had some initial thoughts to share?"

Carolyn nodded, smiling warmly around the room as she stood.

"Thank you, Mr. Wagner," she said to the director, "and, Ms. Pendergrast, it's a pleasure to meet you. On receiving Algus's initial acquisition report last week, I believe there are several areas where we can make an immediate impact . . . ."

Carolyn spoke for about ten minutes, summing up her first impressions of Phossium and what she expected to achieve in the coming months. Board members around the room nodded in approval, occasionally offering up a thought or two. Dolores, too, took extensive notes and smiled encouragingly at Carolyn as she spoke.

The meeting closed with the director thanking Carolyn and once again welcoming her to the team.

As the board members gathered their things and prepared to leave, Dolores walked over to Carolyn, her hand outstretched elegantly in welcome. Carolyn shook it and smiled, marveling slightly at the woman's seemingly effortless air of sophistication.

"Carolyn, dear, it is so nice to finally meet you. I've heard so much about you!" said Dolores.

Carolyn shook her head modestly. "Thank you, though I wish I could say the same about you! I take it from Mr. Wagner that we'll be working together pretty closely."

Dolores nodded obligingly. "Of course, I only began overseeing the Phossium account last month, so I'd be surprised if they said anything to you yet."

She was still holding the tablet she'd been taking notes on during the meeting, and as she spoke, she flicked through a few pages and typed a few lines.

"You know, Carolyn," she said as she typed, "I would absolutely love to sit down with you and 'meld minds' over some of these ideas you have. Of course, we've tried several of them already and not one of them has proven effective, but that's not your fault for not knowing. In fact, I think the first thing I'm going to do is have Phossium's monthly progress reports from the last three years sent to you so you can see what the crew's been up to . . . ."

She typed rapidly for a few seconds, then looked up. "There, done. My assistant will have those reports to you before week's end. Now, as for our meeting . . . ." Once again she consulted her tablet, flicking through her calendar pages. "How does a week from Tuesday sound? 10:00 a.m.? I'll bring tea. That should give you enough time to skim the reports, too, so you can see what's been done. It should help you think outside of the box a little more."

Suddenly, she glanced up at Carolyn with a concerned look. "You won't, I take it, be acting on any of those ideas you shared until we talk, right? I would think you could just take this first week or

LOW-PERFORMANCE LEADERS DRESS REQUESTS AND COMMANDS UP LIKE STATEMENTS.

so to get organized and get settled, then we can work on what needs to happen next."

Carolyn nodded. "Of course, Dolores. That sounds wonderful. I look forward to your insights and thank you for having those reports sent over. I wish I'd thought to ask for them myself," she smiled.

Dolores smiled graciously. "Not a worry at all. I'm glad I can help."

She slipped the tablet into her bag, glanced at her seat to make sure she hadn't left anything behind, then shook Carolyn's hand. "Until next Tuesday," she said.

"Until next Tuesday," Carolyn replied, smiling.

It wasn't until Dolores finally left the room that a vague sense of uneasiness swept over Carolyn, as subtle and inscrutable as the lingering scent of perfume. She couldn't quite put her finger on why, but there was something about Dolores that rubbed Carolyn the wrong way.

After a moment, however, she just shook it off, assigning the feeling to the overall excitement of the day. There were much more important things to focus on, and she couldn't wait to get started.

CHAPTER 3

THE NEW CEO

Despite her excitement, Carolyn took her time walking from the boardroom to her office. There really weren't that many other offices on the fourth floor—a line of empty rooms, dimly lit by the morning sun, could be seen behind the frosted glass walls lining the hallway. Toward her office, she could see the open arch of a break room niche and a handful of closed office doors, the lights on in about half of them.

The smell of brewing coffee caught her attention, and as she veered toward the break room, she almost ran directly into a petite young woman carrying a tray of coffee supplies.

The woman let out an involuntary yelp and backpedaled, the cream and sugar scattering on the tray and the carafe tilting dangerously backward. Carolyn shot her hand out instinctively and caught it before it could spill onto the girl's dress.

"Thank you!" the girl said, quickly sliding everything on the tray back into place.

"No problem," Carolyn said. "Sorry for surprising you like that."

"Oh, it was my fault for not looking where I was going," the girl said, finally looking up from under her dark-brown bangs—and then almost dropping the tray again when she saw who she was talking to.

"Mrs. Qualey!" she started. "I . . . hi! Wow, what an awkward way to meet you. I'm your executive assistant, Bridget Hemsworth. I was just bringing you some coffee."

She offered up an apologetic grin, and Carolyn couldn't help but smile.

"It's great to meet you, Bridget," she said. "And I can tell already that we're going to be a good team; you're already reading my mind! Coffee was exactly why I wandered in here."

Bridget gave her a relieved smile. "Well, I hope you like dark roast. Can I walk you back to your office?"

"Lead the way," said Carolyn.

Carolyn's office was only a few yards down from the break room. The hallway ended with a small door that read "Bridget Hemsworth, executive assistant to the CEO," adjacent to a door on the right-hand wall that read, in fresh gold print, "Carolyn Qualey, Chief Executive Officer."

A sudden rush of pride, undercut by a flurry of anticipation, excitement, and fear, flooded through Carolyn as she read her name with that title in print for the first time—and in gold, no less.

The office was almost exactly how she pictured it. It was a corner space with floor-to-ceiling windows on the outward-facing walls. From where she stood, she could see the cluster of buildings on the other side of the parking lot, the fringe of woods beside the building and the trail that ran along its edge, and in the distance, the glint of a river that divided the city.

A curved, honey-colored wood desk stood to her left, framed by two deep-plush maroon chairs that she had sent to the office. They were gifts from her husband, who'd pointed out that you could positively influence just about any conversation when you have a comfortable place to sit. She couldn't help but agree with him; the wide chairs looked warm and inviting in the otherwise neutral space.

There were a few other personal touches she'd sent in ahead of her, as well: a desk lamp that her son had made for her a few years ago; a few framed family pictures; and on the two center shelves of a built-in bookcase, several of her favorite books, along with her grandmother's personal library. She hadn't read many of Nona's old books, but they held a special place in her heart. Nona had been an adamant reader and had inspired Carolyn as a young girl to do the same, advising her to soak up knowledge "like a morning flower soaks up the sunrise."

Bridget slid the coffee tray onto Carolyn's desk as she looked around.

"Everything look alright?" she asked. "Is there anything missing?"

"It looks great, Bridget, thank you," Carolyn said. "No, nothing's missing. Except for those chairs, I tend to travel light."

"Oh, good," said Bridget. "I wouldn't have put it past the mailroom to misplace a package or two. I mean, just last week they completely lost a shipment of some cardstock that customer relations ordered. Couldn't find it for two days! Man, was old Crespo mad. Of course, he's usually not in that great a mood anyway, but when people start messing with his scheduling, watch out!"

Bridget rambled on as she poured the coffee and adjusted a few pieces of paper on the desk that had been pushed aside by the tray. She looked up at Carolyn as she handed her the steaming mug.

"You'll have to watch your step with a lot of the department heads around here," she added in a confidential tone. "They have their own ways of doing things, and if you mess with that routine, God help you."

"Thank you, Bridget. I look forward to getting to know everyone at this company," said Carolyn. Then, in a more serious tone, she added, "And while I appreciate your honesty, I'd like to get to know everyone here in person first, instead of hearing about them secondhand."

Bridget blushed intensely. "Of course, Mrs. Qualey. I didn't mean . . . that is, I hope you don't think I'm trying to be negative or anything . . . ."

"Don't waste another thought on it, Bridget. You've been wonderful this morning, and I'm looking forward to working with you," Carolyn said. "And speaking of work, it's about time I started digging in."

Bridget smiled and turned to head out. "If you need anything at all, I'm right next door, and my number's on the phone-extension list."

She shut the door quietly, and Carolyn heard a soft series of clicks that told her Bridget had gone into her own office. She sighed deeply. She'd never been a fan of gossip, and while she liked Bridget, she'd have to figure out some way to help her get out of that habit.

I sure hope that's not a regular practice around here, she thought to herself as she took a long sip of coffee and stared down at her desk. The number of things she had to do that day was already stacking up in her mind, so with that thought, she set her mug down, dropped into her desk chair, and flicked on her computer.

WHEN YOU HAVE A SEEMINGLY IMPOSSIBLE MOUNTAIN OF WORK TO CONQUER,

THE BEST PLACE TO START IS AT THE TOP.

When you have a seemingly impossible mountain of work to conquer, the best place to start is at the top, she thought.

CHAPTER 4
LIFELESS

For almost a month before her first day, Carolyn had been collecting ideas about what to do and where to begin at Phossium. She'd dug into online reviews about the company, discovering articles almost two decades old about how successful it had been in its glory days, and then other data sources about how that reputation had slowly decayed over the years, bringing it to where it was now: a document-processing company that survived almost entirely on a handful of legacy clients and a series of one-offs who, on discovering the quality of both the work and customer relations, decided to cancel their services after the first order.

"Survived" might be stretching it, thought Carolyn. According to the internal financial reports, the company had been in the red for almost two years before Algus bought it and hadn't done much better in the three years since then. It was living on life support, and the plug was about halfway out of the socket.

To Carolyn, however, that fine edge was part of the excitement. It would take all of her years of accumulated skills and knowledge to save this sinking ship, but if she could do this, by God, she could do anything.

As she poured through her list of ideas, however, a thought struck her that took some of the wind out of her sails: her promise to Dolores that she wouldn't put any of the ideas she spoke about at the meeting into practice until they met next Tuesday. What was it she'd said? "We've tried several of them already, and not a one has proven effective."

Which of those ideas had failed? Why? Who'd put them into place? The temporary directors that Algus had shuffled through until they found a permanent CEO? How much effort had they really put into them?

Carolyn was kicking herself for not asking more questions earlier, but a promise was a promise, and there were still plenty of things she could do in the meantime. And at the top of that list was something she'd already intended to do as soon as possible: get to know her staff—an idea she hadn't shared at the meeting because, to her, it was a given first step.

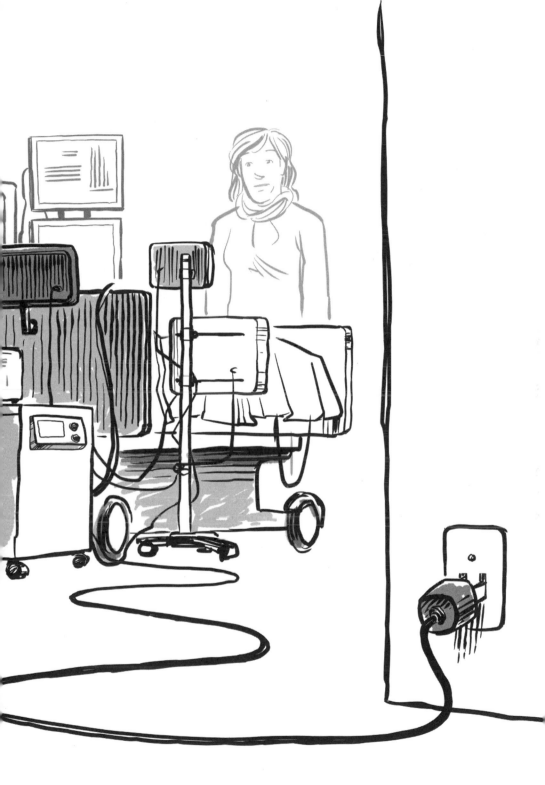

She clicked her screen over to the shared company calendar and began running through the department heads' schedules, selecting open spots and sending invites over the next few days to meet with them individually for a quick introductory chat. And first on that list was the man Bridget had just mentioned: Marsalis Crespo, the head of customer relations.

I guess we'll see if he's as gruff as he sounds, she thought with a wry smile.

The rest of the day saw Carolyn poring through as much of the company's financial history as she could get her hands on, as well as composing an introductory letter to the company's existing legacy clients, which she planned to personally sign and mail out, along with a tin of cookies from a local bakery.

Nothing wins people over like fresh cookies, she thought. She'd give those about a week with each client before calling them with a follow-up. She wanted to make the best impression possible before asking them to share with her their concerns about the company. As for the one-offs, she still had to work out the best approach for bringing them back into the fold, but her head was filled with ideas. The most important thing she needed to do was let them know that this wasn't going to be the same old Phossium anymore. There was a new captain on board, and her intention was to make sure they received the best-quality product and service from here on out.

She was deep into perfecting the wording on the legacy letter when she heard a soft rap at her door.

"Come in," she said.

Bridget poked her head around the corner.

"Just wanted to let you know I'm heading out, Mrs. Qualey," she said.

Carolyn looked at the clock with surprise. It had just hit 5:00 p.m.

"Sounds good. Thanks again for your help today," she said.

Bridget nodded and shut the door. For a brief moment, Carolyn wondered why Bridget hadn't offered to do anything for her before she left, or really, why she hadn't interacted with her much that day at all (although Carolyn had been so deep in her work, she really hadn't noticed Bridget's lack of presence).

It was close to eight o'clock when Carolyn finally shut down the computer, packed up her things, and headed out for the day. The hallways were dark and seemed like they'd

THE SENSE OF LIFELESSNESS WAS PERVASIVE.

HER INTENTION WAS TO MAKE SURE THEY RECEIVED THE BEST-QUALITY PRODUCT AND SERVICE FROM HERE ON OUT.

been abandoned for hours. She took the stairs, and while she thought she heard some sounds coming from the third floor, the whole building had a feeling of desertion.

It wasn't that she expected people to stay late or work the hours she intended to work, but in most productive offices, there were at least one or two night owls to be found working on some last-minute projects. Here, however, the sense of lifelessness was pervasive. It didn't seem like something that should concern her, but that empty feeling haunted Carolyn as she drove home.

The problems at Phossium, she thought, may be far deeper than she'd imagined.

CHAPTER 5

THE RUMOR MILL

The next day, Carolyn arrived at the office right at 7:00 a.m. to an almost empty parking lot and locked front doors. She let herself in, leaving the doors unlocked behind her and turning on the main lights in the foyer. Again, she took the stairs, whipped up a quick pot of coffee in the fourth-floor break room, and headed back to her office.

It was a little after 9:15 a.m. when she finally heard the now-familiar rap on the door.

"Come in," she said.

Bridget stepped halfway into the room, and her eyes zeroed in on Carolyn's coffee mug.

"Good morning!" she said. "Thanks for getting the coffee going. Do you need a refill?"

"I'm set, thank you," said Carolyn. Bridget nodded and was about to close the door when Carolyn stopped her. "Oh, Bridget?" she asked. Bridget swung the door back open. "Yes?"

"Run this letter down to document processing for me, please. I need one hundred copies on our best letterhead stock, and I wasn't sure who would be the best person to ask. I'll need them back by noon."

Carolyn noticed a look of concern cross Bridget's face and raised an eyebrow.

"Is there a problem?" she asked.

"Problem?" said Bridget. "Oh, no, not a problem. Just an impossibility. There's no way document processing is going to get copies to you today. They just don't work like that. They'll put it in the queue, but good luck if you get them in the next two or three days."

Carolyn frowned, and Bridget quickly added, "I mean, I'll ask of course, but to tell you the truth, the people down at DP are about as smart as snails and twice as slow." Her voice lowered as she added, "Personally, I think they spend most of the day just screwing around on the computer. Steven put up this whole tirade on his social page yesterday about global warming, and he must have written it during work, because he posted at, like, 11:00 a.m., and then, like, everyone in the department was commenting on it—"

"Bridget, wait, stop," Carolyn interrupted her, holding up her hand. "That's more than enough information. I'll take this down myself. If they can't get a simple set of papers printed off in three hours, they can tell me why themselves."

Bridget bit her lip and nodded. "If I can do anything else, please let me know," she said as she walked out.

Carolyn gave a small sigh and nodded. "I will, thank you."

Fortunately, Carolyn was already planning on leaving soon for her meet-and-greet with Crespo, so the extra stop at document processing didn't bother her as much as Bridget's need for gossip.

Carolyn pondered the problem as she walked down to the document-processing room on the third floor. There were several offices along the way, most with their doors closed, though she could see the silhouettes of people working behind the frosted glass walls of the larger rooms. One, in fact, with several people in it seemed to have some soft music coming from it, and she could hear a low murmur of chatter. She almost stopped to see whose room it was when she glanced at her watch. She only had about ten minutes to speak with the DP team before her meeting with Crespo, and she was not about to set a bad example by being late.

The main document processing facilities were at the end of the hallway in a large room that mirrored the setup on the fourth floor. A series of industrial printers ran along one wall, and short-walled cubicles filled the space in between. The room was filled with the low hum of scanners and at least one machine running physical prints. No one looked up when Carolyn walked in, so she walked up to the first desk she saw and knocked gently on the wall.

The young man in the cubicle looked up at her quickly, then back at his computer.

"Yeah?" he said as he typed.

Carolyn frowned slightly at the reply, but made herself smile as she replied, "Hi, I'm Carolyn Qualey, the new CEO. I'm looking for someone to help me run some copies."

The young man continued typing, eyes never leaving the screen.

"You'll want to talk to Greg," he said.

"Okay, could you tell me where he is?" Carolyn asked.

He jerked his head backward. "Back there, next to the printers."

Carolyn waited a moment for him to say something else, but that appeared to be the most she would get out of him.

"Thanks," she said.

She walked down the aisle toward the back of the room, reading the small placards on the cubicle walls until she found one that said Greg Mulvaney.

The balding, middle-aged man sitting at the desk was wiping off a pair of round, owlish glasses as she walked up.

"Greg?" she asked.

He looked up, squinting at her, then slid on the glasses.

"Yes?" he replied.

"Hi, I'm Carolyn Qualey, the new CEO. I have something I need printed off and was told to talk with you."

Greg quickly stood up and shook her hand. "Mrs. Qualey! How nice to meet you. I heard you started yesterday and was wondering when we'd get to meet you in person. How has it been going?"

Carolyn smiled. "It's going well!" she replied. "There's a steep learning curve to be sure, but I'm enjoying the challenge."

"Good, good, very good," said Greg, nodding. "Well, what can I do for you today?"

Carolyn handed him a copy of the legacy letter she'd printed out.

GOSSIP IS THE MOST DESTRUCTIVE FORCE IN ANY ORGANIZATION.

"I wasn't sure who to send this to, so I figured I'd print it out. I need a hundred copies of this on our best stock letterhead by noon today. Can you do that for me?"

Greg nodded, looking down at the letter and sliding his glasses up on his nose. "Noon, noon, I see. Rush job. And our best stock letterhead, you say?"

"Yes," Carolyn replied. "Will that be a problem?"

Greg looked up at her, his brown eyes almost comically large behind their round black frames, and glanced quickly around the room. No one was watching them, and in fact, it seemed like everyone in the room had hunkered down into his or her cubicle a little more, as though trying not to be seen.

Finally, Greg looked back at her and nodded.

"I'll take care of it myself," he said, pushing his glasses up on his nose yet again. "Yes, I'll take care of it. Noon? I'll bring them to you. Fourth floor, correct? Corner office next to Bridget?"

"Yes," said Carolyn, nodding. "Thank you so much. I'd stay and chat a little longer, but I have an appointment to get to. But I promise I'll be down here soon to introduce myself to everyone. Thank you again for your help!"

Greg continued nodding, though he was already walking away from her and toward the printers. "Of course. No trouble at all," he said over his shoulder. "I'll have these to you by noon."

Carolyn didn't have much time to think about the strange behavior of the DP team on her way to Crespo's office, though she was glad for Greg; he at least seemed to care about his job, whereas the others almost seemed to be hiding from work.

Crespo's office was one floor below document processing and next to his department's main office. The customer-relations team took up most of the second floor, and as she hurried down the hallway, Carolyn saw several people walking by, though none of them seemed to be in any hurry to get to where they were going. In fact, she had to ease her way around several huddles of employees holding hushed conversations as she made her way to Crespo's, noticing that their whispers dissolved into startled silence as she walked by.

She arrived at Crespo's door just one minute shy of their meeting time and gave herself a little internal pat on the back for keeping her schedule. She knocked promptly on the door and waited for an answer.

Nothing.

Tentatively, she tried the handle. The door was locked, and no light appeared to be emanating from the other side. She looked back down the hallway to see if there was someone she could ask about Crespo's whereabouts, but the huddles had suddenly disappeared, and the corridor was silent. She tried knocking again, but to no avail. Either he wasn't there, or he was so deep in his work that he didn't realize someone was knocking.

Carolyn stood in front of his door for several more minutes, hoping to see him rushing up the hallway and offering his apologies for being late, but all she heard was the low murmur of phone conversations and keyboards clacking in the main customer-relations room.

Finally, she decided to walk over to the second-floor break room and make herself a cup of tea, killing a little more time before she checked one more time. As she was about to round the corner, however, she heard two voices speaking in low tones, one of which had just said, "Carolyn."

"I heard she's a raging bitch," one of the voices, a female, said. "Bridget was telling me yesterday that she never leaves her office and practically snarled at her when she left for the day. What's her deal?"

"I don't know," said the other voice, which sounded male. "I heard she never goes home. I don't think she has a family, or if she does, she obviously doesn't care about them . . . ."

Carolyn couldn't stand the gossip any longer. She took a deep breath and marched around the corner, startling the two employees into stunned silence. She looked at both of them and then extended her hand with a warm smile.

"Hi," she said. "I'm Carolyn Qualey, the new CEO."

The two exchanged a nervous glance and then returned her handshake.

"I'm Delia, customer relations," the woman said.

"Fredrick," said the man. "Same as Delia, customer relations."

ONE OF MY PRIMARY GOALS IS TO MAKE SURE WE'RE ALL **COMMUNICATING CLEARLY AND EFFECTIVELY, BOTH INTERNALLY AND EXTERNALLY.** WE CAN'T WORK WELL TOGETHER IF WE CAN'T TRUST EACH OTHER.

"Delia, Fredrick, it's a pleasure to meet you," said Carolyn. "I do hope I'm not interrupting. I'm meeting with Mr. Crespo shortly and thought I'd grab a cup of tea while I waited."

She began opening cabinets, searching for a cup and the large box of generic tea that the organization kept in stock. As she looked around, she continued, "By the way, I just want you to know that if either of you ever have any questions, please know that I keep an open-door policy. You're welcome to ask me about anything. In fact, you should know that one of my primary goals is to make sure we're all communicating clearly and effectively, both internally and externally. We can't work well together if we can't trust each other."

Finally, she found the mug and tea, filled it with water, popped it in the microwave, and looked back at the two with a smile.

Delia and Fredrick were nodding, carefully avoiding eye contact.

"So please, if there's anything I can clarify for you at any time, I'll be happy to sit down and talk," she added.

"Thank you, Mrs. Qualey," said Delia.

"Yeah, thanks," said Fredrick, who then pretended to check his watch. "Oh, Delia, that call we're supposed to be on starts in five. We need to go."

Delia nodded in relief. "Oh right, I almost forgot. It was great to meet you, Mrs. Qualey. We'll be sure to drop by sometime."

If there had been any dust on the break-room floor, Delia and Fredrick would have kicked up a cloud of it as they scrambled to leave. Carolyn watched them go, feeling guilty for listening to part of their conversation but also angry that the rumor mill in the organization was so fierce. She needed to put the brakes on that habit as soon as possible.

She was still pondering how she'd approach it when she saw a rather round man with a head of thick, curly red hair zip past the break-room doorway in the direction of Crespo's office. She stepped into the hallway just in time to see him disappear behind the office door.

Looks like we've got something to talk about already, she thought, noticing that he was holding his jacket and briefcase as though just arriving for the day. She took a careful sip of her tea and then walked down to his office, knocking gently but with authority.

CHAPTER 6

WHERE CRESPO'S CONCERNED

arsalis Crespo opened the door on her second knock. He seemed surprised at first, then understanding swept over his face.

"Mrs. Qualey, of course. My apologies. I had some errands to run this morning. I hope I'm not too late for our meeting," he said.

It was now fifteen minutes past the hour, but Carolyn simply smiled. Timeliness, she was learning, was obviously not an area of concern at Phossium. She mentally added it to her checklist of "Issues to Address."

"It's good of you to meet with me, Mr. Crespo. You can call me Carolyn," she said, shaking his hand. He smiled, but didn't offer the same informality. He simply gestured for her to come in and picked a stack of papers from a chair so she could sit down. He then circled around to his own paper-stacked desk and took a seat, looking at her expectantly.

Carolyn took the cue.

"As I said in the meeting invite, this is really just a chance for us to formally meet each other and to share your general thoughts about your department. What challenges you've faced recently, positives, negatives, that kind of thing," she said.

Crespo nodded, running stubby fingers through his mop of red hair.

"I see. Well, there's not much to tell," he began. "I've been running customer relations for almost eight years now, and we have a pretty solid system in place. The front line reports to their managers, and the managers report to me. We have three managers right now, and I have no complaints with them."

"And the customers? How are they responding? What's our ratio on converting upset clients into positive return customers?" she asked.

Crespo frowned and began fiddling with a pen on his desk.

"If there's a problem, it isn't with customer relations. It's with the product. What are we supposed to do? If document processing screws up, they screw up. All we can do is say 'Sorry' and offer them a discount on their bill. Of course, we don't do that every time, but in some cases, I'll allow it," he said.

He set the pen down, let out a deep sigh, and leaned his weight back in the chair, propping his elbows on the chair arms and waving his hands about in frustration.

"I've said to them more times than I can count, 'Something needs to be done about the product quality.' But nothing ever gets done. So here I am, managing a bunch of upstart kids who are taking angry phone calls all day and just doing my best to keep this department's head above water," he said. "You want client turnaround? You want people to come back? You talk to document processing. We're too busy with triage."

The look he gave Carolyn was defiant, almost as if he were hoping she would argue with him so he could hammer home the faultlessness of his department a little more.

This is not a fight for today, she thought, reminding herself that she was looking for feedback, not trying to solve any immediate problems. Instead, she nodded and stood up, then reached out and shook his hand.

"I see," she said. "Thank you for your time, Mr. Crespo. I'll be speaking with the other department heads over the next few days and look forward to working with all of you on how we can improve this company going forward."

Crespo gave her a brusque nod. "Good luck," he said, and with that he turned around and began unpacking his briefcase.

Carolyn had been dismissed.

It wasn't quite anger that filled Carolyn as she walked out of the room; more like a combination of frustration mixed with injustice and a touch of hurt pride. Crespo had treated her less like a boss and more like one of those "upstart kids" who worked in his department. He was also monumentally blind as to the entire purpose of his department, which was incredibly worrisome. If his business mind-set was to simply bail out the ship every day instead of fix the holes, this company was sinking even faster than she'd realized.

That impression only grew stronger as Carolyn met with more of the department heads over the next few days. At every turn, she heard the same excuses: "That's not my department," "I've told [blank] a hundred times that something needs to be done about that," "We tried that once, and it didn't work. Why should we do it again?" and on and on. In fact, the only bright spot was when she returned from her meeting with Crespo to find her requested stack of legacy letters printed off, just as she'd asked for them, sitting neatly on her desk.

By Thursday, Carolyn had met with just about everyone, and just about everyone had either been late to the meeting, forgotten about it entirely, or they were completely unprepared to speak with her—unless blaming other departments counted as "preparation." Two of the heads hadn't even bothered to show up at all, and Carolyn had messages out to both for a follow-up, though neither had gotten back with her by the next day.

It was intensely frustrating. The lack of accountability alone was enough to make her scream, even as she struggled to stay composed and open as she spoke with the leaders of her company for the first time. But as she delved more into their inwardly focused mind-sets, she discovered how little they seemed to focus on the true nature of their jobs. Like Crespo, they all seemed to have lost sight of their department's goal. Instead, their idea of "getting work done" was the completion of rote tasks, regardless of the impact on customers.

THEY ALL SEEMED TO HAVE LOST SIGHT OF THEIR DEPARTMENT'S GOAL. INSTEAD, THEIR IDEA OF "GETTING WORK DONE" WAS THE COMPLETION OF ROTE TASKS, REGARDLESS OF THE IMPACT ON CUSTOMERS. JUST AS FRUSTRATING WAS **HER OVERALL IMPRESSION OF WHAT SHE COULD ONLY DESCRIBE AS A "LACK OF PERSISTENCE."**

For instance, Bob Quills, the head of document processing, was adamant that they were completing everything that was given to them to complete. Was it completed on time? she'd asked. Quills had bristled at the question. *We get it done in the time we have*, he'd replied. *Customer relations should be telling them that completion dates have to be flexible because of the nature of what we do. I can't be responsible . . . .* And on and on.

At the same time, she was also discovering how pointless many of the tasks were, such as customer relations reporting on number of client interactions but not the nature of the calls or the results. Or HR spending hours and even days creating internal surveys that only their department ended up taking. Or document processing reporting on the number of projects completed but not on whether they were completed on time or to the customers' satisfaction.

Perhaps just as frustrating was her overall impression of what she could only describe as a "lack of persistence." Easy, repetitive tasks tended to be completed while slightly more complex tasks, such as setting up one of the printers in document processing that had been moved up from storage, stopped the second someone ran into a snag. That printer, for instance, still wasn't online, even though it had been moved four months ago. It was maddening.

After each of her meetings, Carolyn updated her list of "Issues to Address," and by Friday evening, that list was running in excess of thirty pages, single-spaced.

She was just adding the final notes from her last meeting with HR when she heard Bridget's knock at the door. She glanced at the clock: 4:50 p.m.

Seems like she leaves earlier every day, she thought. For a moment, she tried to recall if she'd already added that issue to her list, but her thoughts were interrupted by a second knock.

"Yes?" she said.

Bridget opened the door, a curious look on her face.

"There's a delivery here for you," she said. Behind her, Carolyn could see two men in movers' uniforms holding file boxes.

"Ah," she said, also confused. "Thank you, please let them in."

Bridget stepped aside, and the two men walked in, each with a dolly loaded with boxes. In all, they brought twenty file boxes into the room, setting them up against the far-right wall upon Carolyn's request. As they turned to leave, one of them handed Carolyn a thick, cream-colored envelope with a gold stamp on the back. The front simply read "Carolyn" in a large, looping script. Deeply curious, Carolyn broke the seal and pulled out a matching card with an elegant "D" engraved on the front. Inside, the note read:

> Carolyn – You wouldn't believe our luck! In digging up the monthly reports for the past three years, my assistant came across the entire collection going back to Phossium's founding! I hope you enjoy the read and I look forward to discussing your findings on Tuesday. Sincerely – D

"They're from Dolores Pendergrast?" said Bridget.

Carolyn jumped. She hadn't noticed Bridget standing right behind her, reading the note over her shoulder.

"Looks like it," said Carolyn, snapping the note shut and tossing it on her desk. She walked over to the closest box, Bridget following right behind her, and cut the packing tape with a letter opener. The box was completely filled with papers and one divider tab that simply said "1997". She pulled out a sheaf of stapled documents. "Phossium Monthly Report, October 1997" the cover page read.

"Wow, that's a lot of reports," said Bridget, eying the stacks and stacks of boxes.

Carolyn let out a deep sigh. "Yup," she said. "Looks like it's going to be a long weekend."

CHAPTER 7
THE LAND OF OZ

At times like these, Carolyn was glad her children were grown and her husband was busy with his own work overseas. Otherwise, she would have felt guilty spending the majority of her weekend in her office, poring through report after ancient report as she tried to get a sense of what Phossium was like in its nascent years and the downward-spiraling road it took to get to where it was today.

Since it was the weekend, she didn't bother to dress up, arriving at the office early Saturday morning in her favorite pair of jeans and a loose sweater. She tossed her sneakers off at the door and sat sideways in the chair, socked feet dangling over one chair arm and her laptop perched on her stomach. As she read, she took notes, eventually creating a rough timeline for the evolution of Phossium.

It was fascinating.

Founded by Ozymandias "Oz" Govender in 1985, Phossium was the third enterprise Oz launched in his professional entrepreneurial career. Before that, he'd been a self-employed small-business attorney; and before that, he'd owned three car wash franchises (Carolyn had scratched her head at that one, but *to each his own*, she thought).

The earliest reports appeared to be written by Oz himself, printed out on old dot matrix paper with ink so faded, Carolyn had to squint to read it. His first order, it seemed, came from an associate's law firm, which needed a large quantity of intake forms for a class-action case processed and organized categorically.

Oz had taken care of the entire process himself, working directly with the other attorney to make sure the material was being collated the way he needed it and turning it around in record time. A letter of thanks stapled to the end of the report was filled with words of praise for Oz and how helpful his services had been in making the class action a success.

From there, Oz's order demand grew rapidly, but his focus on the customer was unflappable. Each report included copies of mailed interactions and spreadsheets of phone calls—some to confirm steps in the process, others just to check in, according to the notes. As the demand grew, so did his company. Less than a year after that first order, Oz opened his first location not three blocks from their current office—a small, two-room facility where he apparently kept a desk on the floor right next to his four other employees.

About halfway through his second year in business, Oz included a copy of a small poster in his report. It was written using old-fashioned handwritten calligraphy and included three bold statements:

THE HEART AND GOAL OF PHOSSIUM

WE ANTICIPATE OUR CUSTOMERS' NEEDS AND SURPASS THEM, EVERY TIME.

WE DELIVER UNPARALLELED SERVICE WITH AN ACCURACY RATE OF 99 PERCENT OR GREATER.

WE WILL BE THE NUMBER ONE DOCUMENT PROCESSING COMPANY IN THE COUNTRY BY 1995.

Six months after that, there was a thick addendum to the report containing the paperwork for company health care. Even though there were only six people working at the company by this point, and the prices for health care were steep even by 1987 standards, Oz had signed off on full coverage for all his full-time employees. And once again, the very back of the report included copies of dozens of thank-you letters, many handwritten, from both clients and employees, each expressing their gratitude to him for his services and support.

The upward trend was obvious from that point on, and over the next decade-and-a-half, the company continued to grow rapidly. Oz made it a point to regularly research, purchase, and train the teams on the most cutting-edge document-processing equipment; he continued to build on employee benefits; he kept up his customer-contact schedule with zealous enthusiasm; and the notes of thanks became so numerous that he stopped including copies with the report and just listed their receipt in a spreadsheet.

Then, sometime in 1992, they moved to their current location, where Oz apparently held a huge grand-opening celebration, flying clients in from all corners of the United States and even one from England to join in the official ribbon-cutting ceremony. There were even copies of the press release on the grand-opening event in his report, which was printed in the local newspapers, as well as articles published in three national magazines about Phossium's stellar rise in the entrepreneurial world.

It wasn't until 2000, in fact, that the edges of the company began to fray.

For one, Oz stopped writing the reports. Various names began to appear under the title page, starting with a director of operations and eventually progressing downward in ranks to departmental administrative assistants. The check-in calls with clients all but stopped—or at least, they weren't being tracked with Oz's

former fastidiousness—and the skeleton of a complex internal checks-and-balances system began to appear in the addendums, as though the clear, linear system they'd employed for so many years had stopped working.

At first, the approvals system made sense—who reported to whom, with a straight line from the customer to the approving manager and on to fulfillment—but over time, the structure became more and more convoluted. Red pen marks scratched out various department heads and managers, and turnover began to increase at a rapid rate, which may or may not have had to do with the drastic cuts in employee benefits that began to appear in the notes.

Oz's voice also began to disappear in the reports. Where his influence had been obvious for a while even when he wasn't writing the reports—copies of letters to clients thanking them for their business and his signature on new procedures and equipment purchases—the evidence of his involvement slowly evaporated until Carolyn found almost no trace of him at all.

The last ten years were the most troublesome. The company had continued to grow but had also become increasingly complex. The decision-making process seemed to be revised every month, becoming more and more convoluted, and the high turnover made it difficult to keep anyone with company history and/or talent in a position of authority. Some employees stuck around, of course—she recognized Crespo's name quickly, and Bob Quills in document processing, as well as someone in customer relations named Hugh Walsh, who'd apparently been with the company almost since the beginning. None of those employees, however, seemed to make any significant contributions and generally stayed in the shadows as each month's year-to-date P&L statement continued to dwindle.

> IN THE BEGINNING, OZ WAS IMBUED WITH WHAT THE ENTREPRENEURIAL WORLD REFERS TO AS "FOUNDER'S MENTALITY." **BUT OVER THE YEARS, HE LOST THAT FOCUS.**

In the 2014 reports, she saw the organization-wide announcement of Oz's heart attack and his decision to retire from the company. A few short months after that, another organizational broadcast informed everyone of the upcoming acquisition by Algus Consolidated Systems; and six months later, the reports began to appear on Algus letterhead, written in a highly imper-sonal, structured form that simply highlighted the financial situation of the company and little more.

She finished the last box late Sunday evening, tucking the final Algus report under the handwritten "2017" tab, closing the lid, and collapsing once again into the chair.

It was obvious what had happened.

In the beginning, Oz was imbued with what the entrepreneurial world refers to as "Founder's Mentality." He was right there in the thick of it, obsessing over the customers and making sure they received excellent, unparalleled service. He had grand dreams for the company and shared them with his team, taking the time to have those goals written up and apparently posted all around the office. He'd obsessed about his employees as well, looking out for their well-being and making sure they had the best of the best, both in regard to the equipment they needed and the benefits they deserved.

But over the years, he lost that focus. The red tape of bureaucracy began to creep across the reports' lengthy pages, and the attention to customers was replaced by a greater attention to the bottom line. Employee benefits were cut for the sake of increased profit margins, and equipment funding was slashed for the same reason. System complexity began to kill beneficial growth and, in reaction, the departments cut themselves off from each other, focusing more on saving themselves and their jobs rather than on the organization's original primary focus: the customer.

Carolyn added these final thoughts to her notes, glanced at her watch, and sighed; it was so late, it was almost early.

Wearily she tucked her laptop in the top drawer of her desk, knowing she wouldn't have any time to work on it before she had to be at the office again, and headed home, her thoughts lost in a haze of broken dreams and greatness reduced to dust.

CHAPTER 8
DOLORES

Monday flew by for Carolyn, most of it eaten up with showing Bridget how to package and address the boxes of cookies and letters to the legacy clients, as well as compiling her notes from the Phossium reports and her own notes from her department head interactions over the past week. As it crept closer to ten in the morning on Tuesday, she made sure there was a printed copy of her full report waiting on her desk, and Bridget was briefed on being available at the drop of a hat in case Dolores made any last-minute requests during the meeting.

Then 10:30 a.m. rolled around.

Carolyn pressed the button for Bridget's extension

"Anything?" she asked. Bridget knew exactly what she meant.

"Not a peep," she replied.

Carolyn sighed. "Okay, thank you."

She tapped her fingers on the desk. There was no sense in wasting any more time. If Dolores wasn't going to show up, she had a lot of work to do, and in her mind, if Dolores wasn't

going to keep her promise to speak with her about steps going forward, she didn't have to keep her promise to not take action on her ideas.

She was about to do just that when she heard Bridget's soft rap at the door.

"Come in," she said.

Bridget leaned in. "There's a tea service here for you?" she said.

Carolyn shook her head. She'd forgotten about Dolores's promise to "bring tea."

"Ah, thank you. You can bring it in," she said.

Bridget nodded and opened the door to two women dressed in catering whites, one holding a silver tray with a full tea service and the other carrying a matching silver tea tower, filled to the brim with colorful petit fours. The ladies expertly set up the service on a small folding table they'd brought with them, complete with a white tablecloth, then quietly moved to the back of the room and stood there, waiting.

"Thank you," said Carolyn. "This looks lovely, but I can't imagine we're going to need all this for just two people . . . ?"

The caterers looked at each other and were about to reply when the door suddenly burst open and there was Dolores, impeccably dressed and once again in black, holding her oversized bag and waving her tablet in one hand.

"Carolyn, darling! Oh, I'm so glad the tea is here. What do you think? Did I order enough? These girls run one of the best catering companies in the region, and their macaroons are just to die for. Have you tried one yet?"

She swept into the room, dropping her bag next to one of the chairs and putting her tablet down on the arm. Before Carolyn could react, Dolores was embracing her like an old friend and kissing the air next to both of her cheeks.

Carolyn awkwardly patted her arm in a half-hug and said, "It's good to see you!"

Dolores smiled. "You too, dear, you too. And I'm so sorry I'm late. A few things came up at the office, and then my assistant told the catering company the wrong time. You know how it goes."

She turned around to look at the caterers and gestured toward the tea service. "If you would?" she said, then turned back to Carolyn and sat down in one of the maroon chairs, grimacing slightly at the deeply set seat.

"My, these are interesting chairs," she said, sitting primly on the edge. "You wouldn't happen to have another seat or some pillows perhaps . . . ?"

Carolyn immediately stood up and rolled her office chair over to the tea table. "Please, take this," she said. They switched seats, and Carolyn sunk into the chair, noticing for the first time how much higher someone in the office chair sat than the person in the maroon chair. She'd have to fix that—she didn't want people to think she was trying to be imposing.

Dolores, however, seemed right at home and accepted a cup of freshly poured tea and a plate of baked goods from the caterers. Carolyn did the same, leaning forward as best as she could so she wouldn't appear so far below Dolores while they spoke.

"Now then," said Dolores, "down to business. Did you find those files helpful at all?" she gestured toward the stack of file boxes still looming against the far wall.

Carolyn nodded. "Very. In fact, I think I know exactly how we can start turning things around. Of course, it's going to take time, and we're going to need to do a lot of restructuring and recruitment, but with the right team, this company will really be able to soar."

Dolores arched a shapely eyebrow at her and frowned ever so slightly.

"Now, what do you mean by 'recruit?'" she said. "We already have more than enough people. In fact, I could see clearing out a lot of the lower ranks, and we'd still be fine. In fact, it would help our overall numbers tremendously."

Carolyn shook her head. "I hate to disagree with you, but after meeting with most of the department heads last week, I feel like we would do well to retrain some and replace others. As it is, they're pretty much the main reason this company is being run into the ground right now."

Dolores's frown deepened. "Correct me if I'm wrong, but I felt like we had an agreement. You would not take action on any of your ideas until we spoke today. Why did you meet with the department heads without notifying me first?"

Carolyn gave her a puzzled look. "And I kept that word. Meeting with the department heads was not an idea I'd shared at that meeting. It just made sense that, as the new CEO, I should meet with my team and get to know the current situation a little better."

Dolores typed a long note into her tablet, then set it down and looked up at Carolyn with a somewhat forced smile.

"I understand," she said. "Well, what did you learn overall?"

Carolyn smiled and handed the thick file of her report over to Dolores. "A lot," she replied and immediately launched into everything she'd learned about Phossium, from day one to the present, along with everything she'd learned both through her first week's observations and her direct meetings. She explained the loss of the Founder's Mentality, the deterioration of customer focus, and the growth of siloes between departments. She even added in how the problem of rumors and gossip would need to be cut off at the source if they were going to move forward; how it's difficult, if not impossible, to work in an environment where people whisper behind your back and trust is a lost art.

When she was done, Dolores nodded, flipping through a few of the report's pages as though reading them, and then set the folder down in her lap, neatly folding her hands over it.

"This is excellent work, Carolyn. Thank you for putting this together," she said. "As you've pointed out, and as the Algus team previously identified, we do need to update our systems, though right now, any additional costs are just going to destroy our bottom line. What we need to do is this . . . " She leaned forward as though about to impart confidential information. Carolyn leaned in to hear.

"We need to cut out the fat," Dolores said. "Right now, we have department heads who are willing to work for well below the going salary for their positions, and with less benefits. That's a plus for us. If we get rid of any of them, that not only means some significant salary increases for their replacements, but we'd likely have to revisit our benefits package if we're going to hire on anyone who can do close to the work they're doing now."

Dolores leaned back again, shook her head, and continued, "No, no, my dear. Your intentions are sound, but we have to think about the bottom line. What you need to do is start looking at the riffraff at the bottom and deciding whom we can live without. In fact, my team has already made a tentative list for you of who could be let go without affecting production." With that, she reached into her voluminous bag and pulled out several sheets of paper with names and departments listed on them, some highlighted.

"The highlighted ones are those that I think you could get rid of immediately. To be honest, I'd have done it myself, but now that you're here, I'm sure you can take care of it." She handed the sheets over to Carolyn and then pulled out her tablet again.

THE

CONTEXT

IS

DECISIVE.

"If you would be so good as to let at least ten of these people go by the end of the quarter, I think we could begin looking at some new equipment by . . ." she typed a few numbers into her tablet, "the end of the following quarter." She looked up from the tablet, arching her eyebrows at Carolyn. "Will that be a problem?"

Carolyn scanned the list. She still hadn't met most of the staff but was surprised to see Greg Mulvaney's name not only on the list, but highlighted.

Carolyn wanted to argue with Dolores, explaining to her the old adage, "As the leader goes, so goes the nation," but first she needed to build that argument. These employees could be doing a perfectly good job, but may very easily have been misled by leadership. She would save that argument, however, for another day. For now, she just nodded and said, "I'll see what I can do, Dolores. I understand the priority of making this company profitable again; I just hate to do it at the expense of losing good employees."

Dolores gave her an understanding look that, for just a moment, seemed to teeter on the edge of condescension. "Being a leader is not an easy job, but I'm sure you have it in you. The better we work together, the sooner we'll have this organization in profitable working order."

With that, she stood up, tucked her tablet and Carolyn's report into her bag, and gestured to the catering ladies that they were finished. In a flash, the tea set, tower, and table were packed up, and Dolores was standing at the door. "Until next time, Carolyn. I look forward to a timely update on your progress."

Carolyn nodded, and once again, Dolores whisked forward, grasping Carolyn's shoulders and kissing the air next to both of her cheeks. "Talk to you then, dear. Goodbye."

And just like that, she was gone.

It took Carolyn a moment to process everything that had just happened, and a moment longer to realize that Dolores had just dismissed every last bit of research she'd done over that incredibly long weekend, as well as everything she'd learned from her team interactions. It was as though Dolores had an agenda in mind the whole time and was only humoring Carolyn by letting her think she had some authority.

The thought left Carolyn bristling with anger. She might have even planned that little power move of taking her office chair and sitting above her during that whole talk, too. Carolyn, for her part, hadn't even intended to sit in her office chair; she was going to speak with Dolores face-to-face, comfy chair to comfy chair. And Dolores hadn't even skimmed Carolyn's report. In fact, she wasn't even sure she'd read the cover page.

Carolyn felt an old fire suddenly kindling in her and immediately took a deep, calming breath. *This could all be in my own head,* she thought. *Dolores is busy, and she's a professional. I'm sure she's only trying to help out and save me time.*

Ten people out of a company of more than a hundred wasn't a lot, she reassured herself, and if she could find a way to work with Dolores now, she was sure Dolores would come to see her side of things as well, and they could find a way to rebuild the team structure while still bringing up those bottom-line numbers.

CHAPTER 9

A DESTRUCTIVE FORCE

Fast-forward two months: Carolyn now felt like she was drowning.

Either that, or like she was facing down an entire army with a military complement of one. She was still trying to decide on a metaphor, as if naming it would help. But regardless of how she tried to describe it to herself, the environment at Phossium was feeling more and more like a destructive force.

Having to fire ten potentially good employees was one example, of course. Another glaringly simple one was right in front of her on her desk. It was a simple document-request form she'd created from scratch because she couldn't find an organizational standard for it, or for any other repetitive task.

Later on, she found out that everyone at the company had their own versions of forms, but no one bothered to share them, and the same was true about most tasks. Everyone did things their own way, and employees were practically secretive about their processes. If they found a way to do something more efficiently, for instance, they kept it to themselves.

And that attitude appeared to be pervasive. Every day she overheard superiors harshly criticizing team members for minor failings (such as the failure to use a form they'd never been given), whereas well-prepared reports didn't even receive a "thank-you" and were just as likely to be passed on as a leader's own work.

The gossiping situation, too, still needed to be addressed—as did that list of potential fires from Dolores—but in Carolyn's mind, the more immediate issue was the frustrating lack of shared standards. So, she decided to do an experiment—one that could potentially help her with that list, as well. Once again, she contacted the department heads, including several managers (a few of whom were surprisingly on the Dolores list, even though most of the list was made up of low-ranking members of the organization), requesting they come to a standardization meeting and to bring any forms or written processes that they'd created.

The day of their first meeting, Carolyn was in the scheduled conference room ten minutes early. She'd placed notebooks and pens at each person's seat and had even worked up a quick PowerPoint of the various forms they needed to agree on the structure of or create.

ALIGNMENT PRODUCES POWER.

FRAGMENTATION ERODES POWER.

The time for the meeting came . . . and went. Five minutes passed, then ten. Carolyn stared in frustration at her watch and finally walked over to the office of her director of operations.

"Are you ready to meet?" she asked, taking a deep breath and subconsciously walking through her favorite meditative practice of breathing in compassion and breathing out frustration.

The director glanced up at her from under his headphones and raised an eyebrow, then looked down at the clock.

"Right, sorry. I've been swamped," he said. "I'm on my way."

She found three other department heads and four senior managers the same way, still at their desks and blaming their absence on a heavy workload.

It was almost twenty minutes past the official meeting start by the time everyone sat down, and even then, not a single one of them had the forms she'd asked them to bring. Only one of them, in fact, had really read the meeting agenda, and her excuse was that she "just didn't have the time" to print her forms since she'd received the request a week ago.

"What about everyone else?" she asked. "No time" and "too busy" were all she heard.

"Then we'll talk about this at our next meeting," she said. "You all should have plenty of time to get everything together by next week."

But the next meeting was an almost-painful reflection of the first. Team members began trickling in fifteen minutes late, and what self-created forms and written processes they brought were disconnected and generally useless.

"Stop," Carolyn finally said as yet another manager blundered his way through a half-formed excuse. "Just . . . stop."

She looked down at her hands, which were clenched so tightly that her joints looked like pale pearls against the angry firebrands of her fingertips. She quickly pulled them apart, stretched her fingers out, and then slammed them down on the table. Out of the corner of her eyes, she saw several people flinch in their seats.

She rose, pushing her chair away with the back of her legs, and slowly looked each and every one of the team leaders in the eye. One or two returned her gaze, but most dropped it immediately and stared instead at the glossy tabletop or at some invisible object in the corner of the room. Once she'd made eye contact with each of them, she stepped back and began a slow walk around the table.

"I couldn't tell you exactly what I expected when I walked into this company," she began. "I knew, for instance, that the numbers were down and have been sinking for some time. I knew that there were issues, though on the surface it was hard to tell what they were." She paused and looked around again. Not a single person was looking up at her.

"Now I can see what's wrong, or at least part of it. This," she said, gesturing at the thin stack of hastily scrawled forms in the middle of the table, "is appalling. How do you expect to get anything done like this? Do you even know who's responsible for completing any of these? Do you follow up? Do you even care if these tasks are done?"

She walked up to the director of operations whom she'd rustled from his seat for the first meeting. He'd dragged himself into the meeting fifteen minutes late today, too, though he certainly wasn't the last to arrive.

"Desmond," she said.

He flinched and looked up.

"Can you answer the question?" Her eyes burned a hole through his.

"I . . . um . . . I do care if the work's done, Mrs. Qualey. I mean, that's not really part of my job. It's . . . that is, our departments know their jobs, and we have so much on our plates, we have to assume, you know, that they're doing what they're supposed to do. There are just so many hours in the day . . . ."

He tapered off as the fire in Carolyn's eyes became deadly radiant.

"So many hours in the day?" she replied. "That's your answer? Do you even know what your job is? Do any of you know what your jobs are?" she asked, addressing the entire room.

"Do you? Because if you don't, then the door is right there," she said, pointing. "If one more of you tells me that following up with your team members to ensure the completion of a major task you've assigned them 'isn't part of your job,' then I don't want you on this team. I don't want you in this—and I certainly don't ever want to see your face around Phossium again!"

In a flash, she grabbed the papers off the middle of the table and crushed them in her hands, thrusting them into the trash can next to the door.

"I will follow up with each of you within the week, and at that time, I want to know exactly what you consider your job description to be. And if I'm not satisfied with your response, I will sign your walking orders that day. You are dismissed."

She stood next to the door as everyone in the room left, some avoiding eye contact and others, like Crespo, giving her the cold shoulder. It wasn't until the last one left that she let out her breath and slumped against the wall, the raging fire in her chest dimming to a low, flickering burn. She covered her face with her hands and sighed deeply, willing the peace of meditation to come to her but unable, for the moment, to allow compassion in.

After a minute, she walked back to the conference table and sat down, thinking about what had just happened. She knew she shouldn't have gotten so angry at them, that she'd certainly done more harm than good with that meeting, but with Dolores's list and eye on the bottom line dangling over her, to have the people she was supposed to be working closest with, her leaders, come into a second-chance meeting unprepared, unmotivated, and apparently uninterested in their actual jobs, she had let her temper get the best of her.

She'd put the fear of God in them, certainly, but that was only temporary. On a deeper level, she feared that not a single one of them really cared whether or not this company survived. Across the board, the mentality seemed to be that everyone did the work they were required to do and no more, and even that was done at a painfully slow pace, and any "extracurricular" work requests like asking for help to create a more standardized workflow were ignored. If a task didn't get done, then it wasn't their fault; they weren't the ones tasked with completing it.

There was absolutely no sense of accountability.

GIVING FEEDBACK IS AN OUTWARD EXPRESSION OF LOVE.

CHAPTER 10

THE RIGHT KIND OF FEEDBACK

L ater that evening she was in her office, poring through paperwork, when her cell phone rang. Startled, the first thing she noticed was that it was almost nine o'clock, but then she saw with pleasant surprise that it was her daughter on the line.

"Sadie!" she said with what felt like her first smile all day. "How are you?"

"Hi, Mom!" said Sadie. In the background, music and voices blended into a buzzing, popping hum, but Carolyn couldn't tell if her daughter was out on the town or if it was just another night at her sorority. "I'm great. I just was thinking about you and realized it'd been a while since we talked. How's the new job going?"

"Very well, Sweetie. I mean, it has its challenges, of course, but you know how long I've wanted this kind of a role," she said.

Sadie laughed. "Just about as long as I can remember, that's for sure!"

Carolyn chuckled and then said, "How are classes?"

"Good, Mom, really good. They're tough, but I don't feel too overwhelmed. It's just hard to get any work done when it sounds like this in your room every night."

For a moment, the background noise got louder as Sadie held the phone away from her ear.

Carolyn laughed. "Yup, college is an environment unto its own, that's for sure. And I'm proud of you for putting up with it and focusing on your priorities . . . though that's more than I can say for a few of the people who work here."

"Are you okay, Mom? You sound kinda down all of a sudden," said Sadie.

"Of course, Hon, it's just like I said—it has its challenges. Today, for instance, I may not have handled one of those challenges as well as I could have."

Carolyn went on to tell Sadie everything that had happened between her and her leadership team, from the first meeting a week ago to what happened earlier that day and her angry pronouncement that boiled down to "produce or be put out."

"Well, I don't think you did anything wrong, Mom," said Sadie when Carolyn was done. "But did you do that thing where you tell them they're better than all that?"

Carolyn frowned, perplexed. "What do you mean?"

"Oh, you know, the way you used to talk to me and Augustus. You'd get mad, but you'd also tell us that what we'd done wasn't who we were. That we were better than that," Sadie said. (She was the only one who ever called her older brother by his full name.)

Carolyn slumped back in her seat in shock. What had she been thinking? It was as though the past two, almost three, decades of her life had never happened; that she'd never learned how to provide constructive feedback and she'd reverted, suddenly, to the angry, destructive force she'd been in her early corporate-ladder-climbing days.

Both my kids are out of the house for less than two years, and I've already forgotten everything they taught me, she thought.

"Sadie, you are so right, and no, I didn't say that to them. I don't know what I was thinking," said Carolyn. "I'll speak with all of them tomorrow. Thank you, Sweetheart, you are amazing."

"I know," said Sadie with a giggle. "Let me know how it goes!"

"I will, Sadie-pie. Love you!" said Carolyn.

"Love you, Mom," said Sadie, and clicked off.

Carolyn put down the phone and stared long and hard across the room at nothing in particular, thinking about what her daughter had said and working out how she would tackle making amends the next day—because she'd let too much time pass already.

CHAPTER 11

CONSEQUENCES

The next day, Carolyn went to every single member of Phossium's leadership team who had been at the meeting yesterday and apologized.

At first, when she thought about how she'd make amends, she'd tried to think of what excuse she'd use, what reasoning she had for speaking to them the way she had. But in the end, she realized that her "why" didn't matter to them. What they needed to know was that she didn't think of them as insolent children, which was how she'd come across. Instead, she wanted them to know how smart and capable she considered each of them to be. That she knew they were able to do much better if they put their minds to it.

And that's exactly what she told them. She apologized for snapping, let them know that she wouldn't let it happen again, and that she still wanted to speak with them about their roles, but their jobs wouldn't be hanging in the balance.

Still, despite those brief but honest talks, she received four resignation letters that week from three senior managers and a department head, and one more from another senior manager the following week. Fortunately, the department head resigna-

NO ONE EVER SAID CHANGE WAS EASY.

tion had come from her director of operations, who she learned had been shuffling his responsibilities off onto lower-ranking members of his team for so long that his leaving would have little or no impact. After some quick interviews with a few members of HR, she found a manager to fill the role temporarily until she either found a replacement or the manager proved adept enough at the job to make it a permanent transition.

As for the senior managers, all four were from separate departments, so covering their roles was more a matter of divvying up their responsibilities among the remaining senior managers—a move that didn't thrill the team at first, but she was careful to ensure it was as fair as possible and included a small pay raise for the increased responsibilities. She was sure that wouldn't be a problem with Dolores, as the difference between the raises and what they'd been paying the managers who'd left was negligible. Still, the transition was a rocky one, and she noticed a lot more dour glances in the hallways and hushed conversations in break rooms that stopped the second she walked in.

Consequences of the job, she reassured herself. *No one ever said change was easy.*

CHAPTER 12

THIS IS NOT WHAT A CEO DOES

Two weeks later, Carolyn had only identified two other members of the staff whose jobs could be eliminated with only minor impacts on the rest of the team, which she once again eased with small pay raises to those taking on the greater responsibilities.

Completing Dolores's list of fires, however, wasn't Carolyn's biggest concern, despite the fact that the end of the quarter was rapidly approaching. She had more pressing issues to deal with, one of which was currently filling her computer screen: creating several desperately needed standard forms.

It was something she hadn't needed to do since her college years, when she'd worked as an administrative assistant for a small law firm. But the necessity for standardization at Phossium was obvious: messages were getting crossed, tasks were either being ignored or lost, and what communication there was between departments was fiercely convoluted. Yet no one had ever taken it upon themselves to fix the problem. Again, the lack of accountability was astounding.

"Two and a half months," she muttered to herself. Then a little louder, "Two and a half months as a CEO, and I'm making forms! Ugh!"

Her outburst must have been louder than she thought, because Bridget suddenly poked her head in the door.

"Are you okay?" she asked. "I thought I heard something."

Carolyn smiled and nodded, waving a hand in surrender.

"I'm fine, fine. Thank you. Just talking to myself," she said.

Bridget nodded and ducked back out. Carolyn had considered giving this form-creation task to her, but so far the young woman had only proven useful at taking phone calls and booking appointments. Anything beyond that tended to come back to her either misinterpreted or with items missing altogether. Unfortunately, however, fixing that issue was at the bottom of a very long to-do list.

This is not what a CEO does, she thought to herself for what seemed like the thousandth time that day. The forms needed to be done, and with what remained of her leadership team still on tenuous ground with her, she'd decided to let the forms issue go, take care of the problem herself, and focus on bigger priorities— like getting everyone straight on what their jobs were.

She looked over at the family picture she'd brought from home— the four of them hamming it up for the camera while the surf at a beloved vacation-spot beach rolled in behind them—and thought back to what her daughter had said to her all those months ago: "You were practically running that last company on your own, anyway."

I was running that company, she thought. Back then, the actual CEO had suddenly taken a leave-of-absence for family medical reasons, leaving her in charge indefinitely. Shortly thereafter, the company announced its acquisition by Algus, and it was on Carolyn to make sure the acquisition went smoothly.

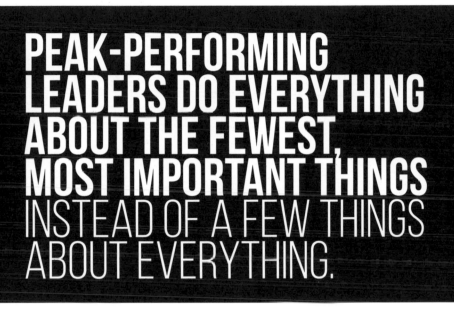

PEAK-PERFORMING LEADERS DO EVERYTHING ABOUT THE FEWEST, MOST IMPORTANT THINGS INSTEAD OF A FEW THINGS ABOUT EVERYTHING.

She'd excelled in the role, but the company had also been in a heck of a lot better shape than Phossium. People had *wanted* to work there. The environment was warm and welcoming, and people offered to help each other at the drop of a hat. She'd loved every minute of her tenure, though she knew it wouldn't last. The CEO was young and certainly not ready to step down, so by the time he returned, she had already begun putting out feelers for a new leadership role—and was thrilled when Algus approached her about taking on another recently acquired company that could use someone experienced in handling organizations during the acquisition process.

Try as she could, however, Carolyn couldn't seem to evoke that warm atmosphere that she remembered so fondly at her old organization, and she couldn't figure out why. The gossiping issue was a problem, of course, but she didn't think there was much she could do about that apart from making it obvious that she didn't approve of the behavior. So along with tackling her day-to-day responsibilities, she'd done things like having doughnuts delivered to all the break rooms on Fridays and replacing the ancient tubs of commercial ground coffee with fresh, locally roasted beans that were ground to order.

Yet, for all her effort, she hadn't even received a single thank-you. In fact, the only thing she heard about either outreach was one complaint: The IT department apparently didn't like chocolate glazed.

CHAPTER 13

MATCH IN THE ROOT CELLAR

Finally done with the forms, Carolyn sent them out to the various departments with clear instructions to use them going forward, even putting that instruction in the subject line in case anyone just decided not to open the e-mail (which was highly likely).

It wasn't the only thing she'd accomplished in two and a half months, not by a long shot, but just the fact that it was needed and no one else had stepped up to the plate to take it on was symbolic of the larger problems she faced with the organization—and finally getting it off her plate didn't make her feel any better. It was like finally chipping a large stone block off the pinnacle of a mountain, only to realize that there was still the rest of the mountain to chip away.

She let herself fall back in her office chair with a sigh, staring dejectedly at the ceiling as she thought about the monumental task she'd taken on. Of course, there was no turning back. She'd worked her whole life toward this position, and the word "quit" had never been a part of her vocabulary. Her concern now wasn't where to go, but where to turn. How could she fix a problem that she couldn't seem to identify in the first place?

As she rolled the question over in her mind, her office door suddenly burst open, and in the split second before the visitor walked in, Carolyn knew exactly who it was.

"I didn't expect much, but I expected *something*," said Dolores as she swept in like a deadly, elegant storm, heels clicking on the wooden floor as she walked up and dropped her black purse squarely in the center of Carolyn's desk.

Carolyn leapt out of her chair and stepped around the desk to greet Dolores, but Dolores already had her tablet out and had perched on the arm of one of the guest chairs.

"It's good to see you again, Ms. Pendergrast," said Carolyn, leaning back against the curve of her desk as Dolores typed away busily.

Dolores nodded, finally looking up with the smile of the long-suffering.

"I'm sorry, Carolyn, I'm just a little flustered today," she said, folding her hands momentarily on her lap. "It's about one week to the end of this quarter, and I've only just heard that you not only haven't addressed that list I gave you, but that we've had several losses in upper management. I'd thought we'd discussed the importance of keeping our higher-ranking officers in place and simply cleaning out the . . . what did I call them . . . the riffraff."

She sighed deeply, then said, "If this were any other employee at Phossium, I would just chalk this up to inexperience and learning the ropes of a new job. But Carolyn, you're the CEO. You needed to hit the ground running, and right now I must say that I'm a little worried that you're not quite up to speed."

Carolyn began to answer, but Dolores had already lifted her tablet up and was reading to her from an open spreadsheet.

"It would also be one thing if the only issue was the discrepancy in who's left the company, but you've also racked up expenses—like these raises—in a short period of time! And what's this astronomical number for purchasing and shipping *cookies*? My dear Carolyn, we're not a bakery. We're not even in the hospitality industry. We are a large *document-processing* organization, and yet you're treating it like your own little boutique shop that you simply run for the tax write-off."

Carolyn's gaze never wavered from Dolores as she spoke, and when she finally looked up from her device, Carolyn leapt in.

"I understand your concern, Dolores, and believe me, I've given that list a lot of thought. And yes, there are some people we could afford to lose on the base level, but I truly don't believe that the first issue we need to address is numbers. If we're going to fix Phossium—and we are—we have to look beyond the bottom line. Not only have we lost sight of our number-one focus—the customer—but there is something pervasively wrong with the entire character of this company. And until we can repair it, I don't believe we can begin to see real, positive, company-wide change—numbers or otherwise."

Dolores's eyebrows lowered, and Carolyn felt the temperature in the room suddenly drop.

"Numbers, Carolyn, are the only real facts of business," she said icily. "If you don't understand this, then it's my duty to report to Algus that they made a rather poor choice in hiring you."

She stood up from the chair and stood in front of Carolyn just a little too closely, looming above her on her sharp heels. Her eyes were cold and hard, but for a moment she allowed her face to soften into a forgiving smile.

"I do like you, Carolyn, you know that," she said, reaching out and grasping Carolyn's arm for a moment in mock sincerity. "Which is why I'm going to give you one more chance. No more unnecessary expenditures, take care of the list I gave you, and if you can make it work without spending another unwarranted penny, you can work on this little morale project of yours. But if I don't see changes in four weeks," her hand tightened ever so slightly on Carolyn's arm, "then I will have no choice but to have you let go."

With that, Dolores tucked her tablet into her bag and turned to leave. At the door, she paused and looked at Carolyn with a wistful look. "I really would hate to see you go, Carolyn. I do hope you'll be able to see the reality of the situation, and soon. I'd hate to replace you. Until next time," she said, and with that, she was gone.

Carolyn let out a deep breath that she felt like she'd been holding for an hour. She closed her eyes and pressed fingers to temples, processing everything Dolores had just thrown at her.

For one, her suspicions were certainly confirmed. That nagging feeling she'd had about Dolores on the first day they'd met was crystallizing into a much clearer understanding of who Dolores was as a person: cold, calculating, single-minded, and immovable when it came to thinking outside the world she'd created for herself. She was fixated on reducing the world to profit and loss, even though that was only one dimension of a far greater picture.

In a way, Carolyn felt sorry for her. Yes, she'd just threatened Carolyn's job, and she could easily have her fired, but as much as that angered Carolyn, it also helped her see Dolores for what she was: a champion of the status quo, a person who would never look beyond the immediate to see the possible. It gave her an extremely limited point of view, but it also helped Carolyn understand a little more about how to deal with her. And that, she decided, was to push her out of her thoughts for now and focus on the bigger picture: What was wrong with Phossium?

Apart from the first and most immediate problem of the loss of the Founder's Mentality and losing sight of the customer, there was also the nagging problem of the lack of accountability and the overall feeling of an environment that was apathetic and broken.

DARKNESS IS NOT THE OPPOSITE OF LIGHT—IT IS THE ABSENCE OF IT.

AND THE SMALLEST FLICKER OF THE THINNEST FLAME, ALL ON ITS OWN, CAN OVERPOWER THE MOST INFINITE NIGHT.

If only she could find the source of the problem, she thought, she could rip it out with both hands and destroy it. But until she did that, she would only continue to find failures in the system. Nothing would work until the whole thing was capable of working toward improvement.

For what felt like the hundredth time that day, she mentally begged the world for the answer to come to her, and as she thought, her eyes fell on the tall built-in bookshelf in the corner of her office. Someone had left a few books on it concerning leadership and organization, all of which she'd flipped through at some point in the hope of finding something helpful, and over the past two months she'd added to it. Along with her own assortment of leadership books were several paperbacks of poetry, a handful of historical and philosophical texts, a few classics, and some dated fiction. The highlight, however, was the two shelves dedicated to her late grandmother's book collection—antique tomes with worn, red leather covers and titles like *The Rose and the Ring* and *The Gentleman from Indiana*.

She glanced at the collection, wondering if one of the books might take her mind off the seemingly impossible task in front of her, when suddenly her eyes caught the gild-script edge of a thin leather pocketbook. *Parables*, read the spine, and nothing else. No author, no publisher. Just *Parables*.

She walked over and flipped through the front pages, looking for a title or copyright page, when a folded piece of paper dropped from the leaves. She bent down to pick it up, carefully handling the thin, aged, and yellowed paper. Unfolding it, she saw that it was covered in a fine, scrawling handwriting that she didn't recognize. An underlined title across the top read, "The Match in the Root Cellar."[1]

"This is a parable of darkness," the script began.

"No night has ever been as dark as this one. There is no moon, leaden clouds mask the stars, and not even the distant, ambient glow of civilization relieves the dark monotony.

"You cannot see your feet, but you know the forest trail you're walking down. You sense the thick columns of old-growth trees, rather than see them, and hear the whisper of leaves on low branches just in time to dodge them. The physical sensation of waving your hand in front of your eyes might as well be the faint memory of a ghost limb for all you can see of it.

"But still you walk on, sensing the path, sensing your steps, and you know without seeing it when you finally arrive at the cabin.

"Your unseen hand fumbles for the door latch, and you walk inside. Somehow, the darkness is even thicker here, and the close air lets you know that no windows, no other external doors except the one you walked in, exist in this space.

"Closing the door, you count your paces until your foot hits an iron ring fastened to the bare floorboards. You reach down and pull it up hard, the rusted iron screeching in its bracket, and swing open the heavy door to the root cellar.

"You walk down, closing the trapdoor above you. The wooden steps sag underfoot, and your hand against the wall brushes

---

1   This parable was originally told by Dr. Rushworth M. Kidder, founder and president of the Institute for Global Ethics. Retold with permission from his widow, Mrs. Elizabeth Kidder.

down dust, dirt, and cobwebs as you walk down, down, down to the hard-packed floor.

"In this earthen pit is darkness unimaginable. It is enough to drive someone mad, enough to hallucinate flecks of false light like distant stars, as though you've somehow been dropped, breathing and whole, on the distant edge of the galaxy.

"And there, in the middle of the moonless, clouded night, in a dense forest, below a windowless house in close dank earth, your hands find a box. But before you open it, you reach into your pocket and pull out a single wooden match.

"The light spits and flares, breathlessly gutters, then holds its flame just as you open the box. As you do, the darkness that pours from under the lid engulfs the room and completely extinguishes the flame.

"Dear reader, is this how darkness works?

"Of course not.

"Darkness is not the opposite of light—it is the absence of it. And the smallest flicker of the thinnest flame, all on its own, can overpower the most infinite night."

The meaning of the parable came to Carolyn in waves, and she stayed in her office long after the building closed that night, letting her thoughts wash over her.

At some point that evening, long after she'd flung off her heels and spun her hair out of the way with a loose, pencil-held bun, she decided to give her husband a call. Although it was late for her, the sun was probably just dawning where he was, making it a good time to catch him.

The video call service chirped softly to let her know it was ringing in his hotel room, some six thousand miles away, and after a long minute, he finally picked up.

"David?" she said.

"Hi Hon, how are you doing?" he said.

She could see that his thick salt and pepper hair was still damp from the shower and that he was buttoning a pale-blue oxford over his standard undershirt; she could almost smell the woodsy scent of his aftershave. Carolyn smiled.

"I'm well, Hon. It . . . it's been a rough day. Hell, it's been a rough month," she said, and suddenly, without really thinking about it, everything came pouring out of her—about the company, the financial situation, the people, the disconnectedness, Dolores. . . all of it. She'd spoken with him before about her job, but those calls had been quick recaps just to make sure they didn't lose touch with each other. This time, however, she let it all out.

On the other end, David listened without interruption and gave her a moment to collect her thoughts when she was done. In that silence, Carolyn realized that she'd been staring at her hands for most of the call, which she'd clenched unconsciously into white-knuckled fists. She forced her fingers to relax and looked up at

David with half a smile. He returned it, but his brow was knit with concern.

"So that's it, huh?" he asked.

She gave a short, sharp laugh, "Yeah, I guess that's it." Then, with a start, she began rapidly searching her desk.

"No wait, that's not it," she said. "I mean, yes, that's what's been going on, but it's not the only reason I called. I found this, and I think . . . I feel like there's something here, something profound . . ."

She finally found the handwritten parable, half-tucked away under her laptop, and quickly pulled it out.

"Ah, here we go. I have no idea who wrote it, but listen to this," and she read the short parable to David in its entirety. Once again, when she was done, David remained silent.

"So, what do you think?" she asked.

Oceans away, David shook his head.

"It's not what I think, it's what *you* think," he said. "Obviously that parable spoke to you. What did it say?"

And finally, for the first time since she started at Phossium, Carolyn was able to put her situation into words. "The darkness in this parable," she explained, "is the same darkness that this organization is immersed in. This apathetic, spiritless environment isn't some disjointed, impossible puzzle

to solve; it's a void to be filled, an absence in need of a light. It's not an issue of these thousands of individual, unrelated, impossible-to-solve problems; they're just parts of a greater whole. It's all one giant *absence*—the absence of light; the absence of a positive culture; the absence of the *best* culture we could possibly have!"

It was a challenge that she'd never had to name before, because she'd never encountered its negative side to this degree, but now that she thought about it in this way, now that she knew what to call it, she could figure out how to repel it.

"David, thank you," she said. "Thank you so much for listening. I think I just needed to talk this out, and now . . . my God, I have so much work to do!"

He laughed. "Glad I could help! And hey, Babe . . . call me sometime, and we'll catch up more. I know you have to run, but there are a few things I want to tell you about this project I'm working on right now. It's amazing, but some of the things we're dealing with sound like they might relate with your situation. Think we could compare notes?"

"Of course, David, I'll call soon. Thank you again. I love you," she said with a smile.

"Love you," he said, and hung up.

Carolyn was barely off the call when she began typing.

THE PROBLEM
WAS THAT

PHOSSIUM HAD NEVER DECIDED ON WHERE TO SET THAT LINE.

CHAPTER 14
NAMING CULTURE

There really is a power in naming something, she thought. In identifying the issue as "culture," she suddenly saw the threads that tied together so many of the seemingly intangible challenges she was facing.

It wasn't that culture, in itself, was a good or bad thing, she realized. It was simply an unspoken line that had been drawn by everyone in her organization. Anything that fell above that line was acceptable, and what fell below that line wasn't.

The problem was that Phossium had never decided on where to set that line. Instead, the line had grown slowly, mold like, into place, feeding off rotten behaviors like back-biting, apathy, and lack of accountability, because no one cared to stand for anything more.

It was a default culture, permitted by every last member of her company, from the mail clerk to herself, the CEO, and as much as she wanted to be the hero who swept in and single-handedly eliminated the old line and drew a new one at a level that encouraged things like kindness and motivation, and discouraged gossip and apathy, she understood that she could only be the first match. She would need others to get behind her, sharing their light until the darkness was eliminated.

But she also knew that just attacking the symptoms didn't eliminate the cause. First, she had to follow the symptoms of Phossium's default culture back to its roots, discover the cause, and destroy it at the source so the problems would go away for good.

So, the question was, at what point had the Phossium culture begun to deteriorate? What was the root cause?

CHAPTER 15

SEEING THE FOREST

After a while, Carolyn stood up from her desk and took a slow, barefooted walk around her office. It was well into the evening, but the only light on was the warm glow of her favorite desk lamp—a gift from her son when he'd decided that he wanted to become a metalwork artist.

She'd had her doubts about his decision, just as she'd had when he told her that he was definitely going to become a pilot, and before that, a poet. But she encouraged him and let him discover himself, and he'd impressed her every time. As a poet, he took the time to write, edit, and publish a lovely, thoughtful collection. It was never picked up by a publisher, but the fact that he'd followed through with it was more than she could say for many would-be authors. As a pilot, he'd graduated from a professional pilot program before deciding it wasn't right for him.

With metalwork, too, he'd taken the time to learn several of the art's intricacies, from arc welding to forging to glasswork. The lamp, in fact, had been his journeyman piece. She'd been so proud of him when he presented it to her, an awkward, hopeful smile on his face as though he still hadn't decided if the piece was any good. She'd hugged him, tears in her eyes, and thought that maybe he'd found his calling this time. It was truly beautiful. But, that skill learned, he'd moved on to tackle another art form that was surprisingly holding his interest to this day: medicine.

She ran her fingers over the fine lead welds of the shade. What had most impressed her wasn't so much what he'd created, but that he'd kept his word. He'd wanted to learn, so he did, and he followed through on every one of his promises.

The thought suddenly struck her out of the blue.

She leapt back onto her laptop and began typing as fast as her thoughts came to her, the words pouring out almost too fast for her to type.

The root causes of Phossium's default culture were right there, glaringly obvious but hard to see when she kept separating the issues in her head, such as rudeness versus indifference.

I just couldn't see the forest for the trees, she thought.

The causes initially weren't coming to her as single thoughts, but rather as distillations of poor-culture incidents that she'd observed over the past few months. Boiled down, they became two obvious, interlocking causes:

- **Not Keeping Your Word**
- **Giving Up**

Immediately under those, she typed out the answer:

- **Integrity**
- **Be Your Word**
- **Be Intentional**
- **Be Persistent**

It was deceptively simple. Of course, the answer to people not keeping their word was to make it unacceptable to go back on your word, but getting enough people on board so that keeping your word became as natural as, say, blinking, was another thing entirely.

All we have to do is start, Carolyn thought, remembering her mountain-chipping analogy. Once the new culture—a culture where everyone was motivated to work at peak performance—began to catch on, it would spread more and more quickly. Carolyn ran a hand through her hair as she read back through everything she'd written. At one point, she glanced at her watch. *Good lord*, she thought, *it's late enough to be 'early!'*

She looked back at the screen. She'd done all she could for now. Tomorrow—or rather, later that day, according to her watch—she'd take the first steps. Not only would she actively stand for

a better culture, a culture that actively encouraged and celebrated the peak performance of her entire team, but she'd also
find others who would stand with her.

The beginning of the next workday had suddenly become as
important and exciting to her as that very first day at Phossium,
only a few short months ago. All thoughts of Dolores and her
dark threats left her. This was the
change she'd been looking
for. *Better, actually*,
she thought, *because
tomorrow, we're going
to change the world.*

CHAPTER 16

BE YOUR WORD

"When we try to pick out anything by itself, we find it hitched to everything else in the Universe."

JOHN MUIR

———

Change the world.

That thought had stayed with Carolyn the rest of the night, burning in her with an excitement that she hadn't felt in months—because it was true! Changing the culture at Phossium—raising the line and imbuing her team, her organization, with the courage to want nothing but the best from themselves and from others—was not going to be a localized event. That passion would feed into every one of her team members' lives as they realized the deep, almost visceral importance of living by your word and doing what you say you're going to do, no matter what, persistently, and without fail.

Other people couldn't help but notice that kind of attitude, that unspoken demand for the best from oneself. For someone who persisted in standing by those conditions, to do any less was to instantly see his or her own failings . . . and want to do better.

It was as though all of the things she'd tried to stand for in her own life—with her career, her children, and with her marriage—had suddenly become physically tangible. She knew she wasn't perfect, but to name what she stood for—Be Your Word, Be Intentional, Be Persistent—was to make them fiercely and undeniably real.

She walked in the front door at Phossium at the same time she did every day, greeting the young man at reception in what she felt was the same way she always did, but instead of the silent chin-tilt-of-acknowledgement that she usually got, he seemed startled and looked up at her with curiosity.

> IT WAS AS THOUGH ALL OF THE THINGS SHE'D TRIED TO STAND FOR IN HER OWN LIFE—WITH HER CAREER, HER CHILDREN, AND WITH HER MARRIAGE—**HAD SUDDENLY BECOME PHYSICALLY TANGIBLE.**

"Good morning, Mrs. Qualey," he said. "Are you doing okay today?"

"I'm great, Jeff," she said with a laugh. "Just great. Today is going to be a fantastic day."

She punctuated the statement with a light slap on his desk and successfully fought the urge to skip a little as she turned down the hallway. She felt utterly vibrant.

CHAPTER 17

THE FIRST MATCH

arolyn was just about to swing through the stairwell door when she caught the tail end of a conversation coming from one of the nearby offices.

". . . don't care. This was your project, and it was on you to complete. You haven't done it, so what do you want me to do about it?"

Carolyn stopped in her tracks. Here was her first opportunity to kick-start this culture of peak performance. She turned around and quickly found the source of the conversation three doors down, in the office of a customer-relations team manager.

The door was wide open, framing both manager and team member. The manager, a long-time Phossium employee whom she'd met briefly last month during a departmental meeting, was slung so far back in his chair that it looked like it might tip over, his hands folded over his sweater-vested potbelly as he stared at the young woman in front of him with both annoyance and contempt. The team member, dressed conservatively in a short-sleeve blouse and A-line skirt that hugged her waist, looked nervous but resolute, a sheaf of neatly bound and tabbed papers clasped in her hands.

Both of them looked surprised when Carolyn gently knocked on the doorframe.

"I'm sorry to interrupt," she said, "but I couldn't help but hear part of your conversation from the hallway."

The manager's chair screeched painfully as he pulled himself to his feet and gestured for her to come in.

"Not at all, Mrs. Qualey, please come in," he said. "I hope we weren't being too loud."

She shook her head.

"No, you're fine, Mr. Walsh. It wasn't the volume that caught my attention, it was the topic," she said, and then she turned to the team member. "I'm so sorry, but your name has completely slipped my mind."

"Batya, Batya Cohen," she said, reaching out to shake Carolyn's hand. "No worries at all. We only met briefly after you started here. I imagine you have a lot of names to remember."

Carolyn shook Batya's hand and nodded, grinning. "I do, but that's no excuse. It's good to meet you again, Batya. Now, if it's not a matter of confidentiality, could you tell me what you were discussing?"

"Of course," said Batya, glancing quickly over at Walsh for his approval. He nodded stiffly.

Batya continued, "About a week ago, Mr. Walsh tasked me with solving an external-communication problem that needed to be handled pretty quickly. I reviewed it, and, to me, it looked like something that could be solved much more quickly if I got more people involved, so I formed a team with three others in the department. Together we came up with four different possible causes, and each of us decided to take on one of them, and we all agreed to meet up again in a week to discuss our results.

"A week later, not a single one of them showed up to the meeting," said Batya, glancing over again at Walsh, who was now expressionless. "I walked to their desks to ask them about it, but each of them told me that they'd had something else come up and didn't have a chance to look at it.

"I did what I could to finish the report without their input, but it was due today to Mr. Walsh, and I had to be honest with him . . . it's not as thorough as it could be."

Batya had been glancing down at the thick report in her hands while she was speaking, and from where she stood, Carolyn could see the handwritten notes and highlights on what looked like a very detailed analysis.

Walsh gestured at the papers in Batya's hands. "Kids today, you'd think they expected the world handed to them on a silver platter," he said. "If the others didn't do the work, that's Batya's fault. It was her job to begin with. To me, that's automatic failure."

Batya looked up at Carolyn, that resolute look once again in place. For the first time, Carolyn saw past the frame of Batya's dark-framed glasses to the deep circles under her eyes, the rumpled blouse that appeared to have been slept in. Batya didn't look like she'd left the office in a week, and she suspected that this report was the reason why.

"May I see your report, Batya?" She asked.

Batya nodded and handed it to her. One look immediately confirmed Carolyn's suspicions: It was almost 125 pages of carefully thought-out strategy, with handwritten notes on each page asking further questions, elaborating on thoughts, and positing other possible alternatives. *It wasn't complete, because she hadn't answered every question that occurred to her*, she thought. *But this looks like one of the best reports I've seen come out of this company yet.*

"Thank you, Batya," she said, handing the report back to her. "Mr. Walsh, I'd like to speak with you a little later. Batya, do you have time to talk?"

"Yes," she said, glancing down at her watch. "I have a few hours before my next meeting. What can I do for you?"

Carolyn nodded. "Good, we can talk about it on the way to my office."

As she turned to go, she nodded quickly to Walsh.

"And thank you for your time, Mr. Walsh," she said.

"No problem at all," he replied, his expression still stony and dark.

IF THINGS ARE GOING TO CHANGE AROUND HERE, **WE NEED TO GET MORE PEOPLE THINKING LIKE YOU DO.**

As she and Batya walked down the hall to the stairwell, Carolyn congratulated her on the report. "It's really well done," she said. "I'd like to take a closer look at it, but from what I saw, you've done a very thorough and thoughtful job."

"Thank you," said Batya with a small smile.

"And I understand what happened to you with your teammates all too well," she continued. "In fact, I'd like to talk with you about that specifically, because I believe you can help me keep things like that from happening again in this organization."

Batya nodded. "I'm honored. Thank you." She paused for a second, unconsciously pushing her glasses up on her nose before saying, "And I'm also very curious. A minute ago, Mr. Walsh sounded like he wanted to fire me. I didn't complete the report, so . . . should I be worried?"

Carolyn stopped walking and turned to her with a smile. "Batya, I need you in this organization more than I need just about anyone else right now. Before today, I didn't believe anyone in this company believed in the importance of standing by their word. Today, you demonstrated to me that you do; that you will do everything in your power to finish what you say you're going to finish, and to do what you say you're going to do. There are few things in this world more powerful than that.

"If things are going to change around here, we need to get more people thinking like you do," she added. "Which is why I've asked you to join me. I have some ideas I'd like to run by you."

CHAPTER 18

BE INTENTIONAL

"Every man's life represents a road toward himself."

HERMANN HESS

———

I t only took about half an hour for Carolyn to tell Batya every-thing she'd learned about the culture at Phossium: from the challenges she faced with timeliness to the overall inclina-tions for gossip, self-serving actions, and a silo mentality.

"Integrity is vital," Carolyn concluded, standing up from her office chair to lean against the desk for a moment. "We cannot, as individuals, perform at our best if everyone else isn't performing at their best, which means that if you give your word, you stand by it, no matter what."

Batya nodded. "So that's the first step. That's why we need to get everyone on board before we do anything else."

"Right," said Carolyn, "which is why your challenges with that problem-solving team, and with Mr. Walsh, make you ideal to help get this going. You're already living with integrity and expecting others to do the same. I can't get this going alone, and I certainly can't make people do it 'just because I'm the CEO.' The desire to change, to live with integrity and be your word, can be exemplified by a boss, but I believe it's driven even more by peers."

Batya shook her head. "I don't know how much influence I'd have. I've been here a little over a year, and there are people on my own team who don't even know my name. Why would they care what I do or don't do?"

"Because, whether they realize it or not, you will be leading them," said Carolyn. "Before today, you lived with integrity naturally, but you probably didn't assert it much with others. If someone failed to keep his or her word, you probably just let it slide, right?"

"Sure," she said, looking down.

"And you've probably taken on more than you could handle just to make others happy, and not only exhausted yourself, but failed to do as good a job as you could have on that excessive pile of projects, right?" said Carolyn, glancing briefly down at Batya's report.

Batya clenched her jaw a little as she nodded again.

"That stops today," said Carolyn. "Today, if you're willing and if you're strong enough—and I truly believe that you are more than strong enough—you will commit to standing by your integrity and making it known that you expect the same from others. And you become *intentional* about it."

What this meant, Carolyn explained, was to live by three essential codes of conduct:

1) When you give your word, stand by it—regardless of how insignificant that "word" may seem.

2) Say "yes" only when you mean it.

3) When you do say "yes," defend it. If agreeing to do something compromises a promise you made earlier, then don't agree to do it. Stay true to your promises.

"Your word," said Carolyn, "could mean anything from agreeing to give someone five minutes of your time to agreeing to turn a project in by the deadline or showing up to a meeting when you say you're going to be there. It's something to be held sacred, and, ultimately, it's one of the few things we have in this life that we are free to give. It is the single element that allows others to build trust in you . . . or not."

Standing by your "yes" is integral to that, Carolyn explained. When you say "yes," others expect you to follow through. If you don't follow through, you lose trust; you're no longer your word. For that reason, saying "no" is just as important. If you agree to one thing, and saying "yes" to something else compromises that first promise, you are bound by your word to say "no," instead.

"It all comes down to 'trust,'" said Carolyn. "When we do what we say we're going to do, people begin to trust us. It's the purest, most elemental basis for any relationship. Without trust, how can anything else exist?"

Batya nodded. "If we don't have trust, we have nothing, and if people don't believe us when we say we're going to do something, then we can't build trust to begin with. But it's not a natural thing, right? That is, it's something we have to remind ourselves to do . . . right?"

Carolyn smiled. "Right. As humans, we're naturally inclined to look out for ourselves first. We'll want to do what's in our own best interest before anything else, even if that means going back on our word. It could be as simple as promising to call your parents over the weekend and then not doing it because you got wrapped up in some television marathon, or something more obvious, like not finishing a report on time for the same reason."

Batya laughed a little and then looked serious. "I've certainly forgotten to call my parents more than once, but when you put it that way, I feel terrible. How many other times have I gone back on my word?"

"That's where 'being intentional' comes in," said Carolyn. "Like I said, we're all human. We've failed in the past, and we're going to fail in the future. I know there have been times when I haven't called my family either, even when I said I was going to. But if we're intentional about being our word, and remain conscious of it every time we give it, then we're much less likely to fail . . . and far more likely to live with integrity."

Carolyn paused for a moment before saying, "In fact, there's a very clear way we can acknowledge those failures when they happen."

IT ALL COMES DOWN TO TRUST.

MATCH IN THE ROOT CELLAR

CHAPTER 19
ACKNOWLEDGING A BREACH

Carolyn leaned forward and walked back to her desk where she quickly jotted down a few notes. When she was done, she spun the laptop around so Batya could see. Across the top, Carolyn had written "Breach: When We Fail to Be Our Word," under which she'd written three points:

1) **Acknowledge the breach**

2) **Reestablish your integrity**

3) **Offer the gift of forgiveness (optional)**

"Notice what's here and what isn't here," said Carolyn. "What's here is personal acknowledgement and a clear reestablishment of integrity. What's not here is an excuse. Excuses are simply a waste of time, and really, no one cares about them."

"So, if I was late to a meeting," said Batya, "not that I would be, but if I was, I would clearly acknowledge what I'd done. I'd say, 'I said I would be here at 9:00 a.m., and I was not.' Right?"

Carolyn nodded. "And to reestablish your integrity, you simply say something along the lines of, 'In the future, you can depend on me to do what I say.'"

"Got it," said Batya. "But why is forgiveness optional? And why is it a *gift*?"

"Because the person you affected with your breach can still harbor negative feelings toward you, regardless of your acknowledgement. By asking for forgiveness, you're giving them the opportunity—the gift—of letting those negative feelings go for good," she said. Then, with a start, she added, "And speaking of forgiveness, there's someone I need to talk to."

Batya smiled and got up. "I'm not sure who you might need to acknowledge a breach with, but best of luck. And as for improving the culture here, I know you know this, but it isn't going to be a walk in the park. Not everyone is going to like what we're doing, or even agree."

"Oh, don't I know it," said Carolyn with a wry grin. "That's why we can't give up—and we need to get more people behind us as soon as we can. This new culture isn't going to happen quickly or easily, and even when we do make it happen, we can't slack. We need to stand for it every day. But I'm up for the challenge. Are you?"

Batya laughed. "With that kind of stump speech, how can I say no?" She smiled and shook her head. "Of course I'm up for it. This is something I've wanted to be a part of for a long time . . . I just never realized it until we spoke today. Let's do this."

CHAPTER 20

BE PERSISTENT

> "Until one is committed, there is hesitancy, the chance to draw back . . . Whatever you can do, or dream you can do, begin it. Boldness has genius, power, and magic in it. Begin it now."
>
> **WILLIAM H. MURRAY, SCOTTISH MOUNTAINEER AND AUTHOR**

The door to Walsh's office was closed, so Carolyn stood outside quietly for a moment to make sure he wasn't on the phone or holding a private meeting. To her surprise, the only sound she heard was a low, beautiful female voice singing a sultry version of "Tenderly."

She hesitated another moment and then knocked.

"What?" said a gruff voice on the other side. The music suddenly cut off mid-song.

"Mr. Walsh, it's me, Carolyn. May I come in?" she said.

There was the prolonged squeal of a desk chair and a few shuffled steps before the door opened. Walsh looked the same as he had about an hour before, except that his tie was perhaps a little looser around his neck.

"Mrs. Qualey," he said, standing in the door and staring at her with a barely concealed frown.

"Mr. Walsh," she replied. "I was wondering if I may come in? I'd like to speak with you about earlier today."

Walsh's watery blue eyes narrowed, but he stepped back and gestured for her to enter the room.

"Thank you," she said. She looked around for a guest chair but couldn't spot one in the stacks of papers, file folders, and sundry unused office equipment that lined the walls of the small room. Instead, she opted to stand casually with her hands clasped gently behind her back while Walsh found his way back to his seat.

The chair groaned as he sat, leaned back, and looked up at her with the same glint of half-veiled annoyance. After a few seconds of silence, Carolyn decided to start the conversation.

"Mr. Walsh—may I call you Hugh?" she began.

Walsh shrugged, though he seemed surprised that she remembered his first name.

"Hugh—and please call me Carolyn—I want to acknowledge what I did earlier today. I understand that it was not my place to interrupt a supervisor correcting a team member. It won't happen again," she said.

Walsh continued his stony silence, but Carolyn let it be this time. A few moments went by before he finally spoke up.

"Is that all?" he asked.

"If you're busy right now, then yes. But if you have a minute, I'd like to speak with you a little more."

Walsh looked for a moment as though he was searching for an excuse to ask her to leave, but stopped himself. "I have a few minutes," he conceded.

"Thank you," said Carolyn. She gathered her thoughts for a second and then said bluntly, "You don't like me much, do you?"

Walsh's eyes widened. "I wouldn't say that . . . Carolyn," he said, the casual first name a little difficult for him to get out. "I 'like' you as much as I like anyone else at this company."

Carolyn gave a short laugh. "I don't know if that's a good or bad thing."

Walsh didn't smile, but his frown became a little less severe. "What I mean is, I don't know you very well at all. You seem to want to do well, but to be honest, we've had very little interaction up until now."

"Of course," said Carolyn, "and I understand that. That's something I want to address, as well. But ever since we met during my first week here, I've had the impression that you don't quite approve of me."

Walsh leaned forward in his chair and put his arms on his desk. "It's not that I don't approve, Mrs. . . . Carolyn. It's that things here . . . well, things here were just fine until you and that Algus group moved in. We had our way of doing things. Maybe it's not everyone's way, but it was working for us. Now you come in here with your bright ideas on processes and paperwork and meetings and . . . it's just not us. It's not Phossium."

Carolyn rocked back on her heels and was about to reply when she suddenly spotted a couple of empty milk crates in the corner of the room. "May I?" she said, pointing at the dusty pile, and before Walsh could reply, she'd picked them up and dropped them beside his desk. She sat down on them, ignoring the dust, and leaned forward, looking him right in the eye.

"No," she said. "It's not Phossium. But whether you want to admit it or not, Phossium is failing. I don't want that to happen, but for this company to survive, we have to change. And I would like you to be a positive part of that."

She leaned back on the crates for a moment and then said, "Tell me, Hugh. How long have you been here?"

Walsh shrugged again. "Twenty-nine years this December."

"I thought you'd been here a while, but I didn't realize it was so long," she said.

"Yup," he said. "Phossium was a little over two years old when I started here as a mail clerk under Oz Govender, the former owner. Talk about a dying breed. Oz was one of the best bosses a kid could have . . . ."

Walsh leaned back in his chair as he warmed up to the story, and Carolyn found herself learning even more about the company than what she'd gathered from the monthly reports. It was Phossium's history come to life, and through Walsh's memories, she also gained an important insight into the reason behind the company's culture issues. It all went back to that Founder's Mentality. As it was lost, the culture began to fall apart as well.

From the old reports, she'd gathered that Oz had slowly lost interest in those elements that made him so successful in the beginning: his insatiable focus on the customer; his drive to cut straight to the chase and avoid bureaucracy; and his desire to ensure his employees were taken care of. Walsh didn't say it in as many words, but he alluded to Oz's withdrawal from the organization and the loss of the "soul" of the company that went with him. And as operations fell into the hands of "newcomers" (he said this with a sidelong look at Carolyn), the soul of Phossium also slipped away.

Through it all, however, Walsh had stood by Oz and Phossium, rising slowly through the ranks and fighting for every step. Oz may have liked Walsh, and Walsh certainly looked on Oz as a kind of father figure, but Oz had also apparently been a firm believer in earning everything one got in life—a mentality that Walsh took to heart. It took more than a decade for Walsh to become a customer-relations manager at Phossium, and because of this, he didn't believe anyone deserved a "helping hand." Team members either earned their place at the company or they didn't. At least, that was what Carolyn surmised from Walsh's memories of late nights, impossible workloads, and hard-earned pats on the back.

The regression to a default culture at Phossium wasn't entirely due to Oz and his slow disappearance from the organization, but that certainly contributed to it. And Carolyn had a sneaking suspicion that the degradation in the quality of operations managers had helped with the rest.

"But enough about the past," Walsh said suddenly, startling Carolyn out of her thoughts. "What's done is done. You're here and old man Oz is out enjoying his retirement, probably somewhere well south of here. You didn't come here to listen to me reminisce."

Walsh raised a bushy, questioning eyebrow at her, and Carolyn smiled as she stretched out a little from the listening hunch she'd assumed on the awkward crates.

IT ALL WENT BACK TO THAT FOUNDER'S MENTALITY.

AS IT WAS LOST, THE CULTURE BEGAN TO FALL APART AS WELL.

"You're right, though you just taught me more about Phossium in twenty minutes than I've been able to learn with a whole lot of digging," said Carolyn appreciatively. "I actually got to two of the three things I wanted to talk with you about when I walked in, and I couldn't get to the last one until I did those: acknowledged my failure to you and confronted you about your initial perception of me and my role.

"Item three," she continued, "concerns integrity."

For the second time that day, Carolyn walked through her revelation about the culture at Phossium, being careful to describe the current state in terms of fact instead of perception and belief. Still, Walsh's eye would occasionally twitch, or his frown would become more perceptible as she touched on sensitive subjects. But she powered through, taking him through the insights she'd gained both on her own and through talking with Batya.

When she was done, she returned his questioning eyebrow, arch for arch.

"So, what do you think?" she asked.

Walsh leaned back in his chair, which protested loudly.

"I don't agree with everything you said, and some of what you said about what's going on around here is just wrong, but I can appreciate where you're coming from . . . especially when it comes to keeping your word," he said. He paused a moment, then continued, "I can also see that this isn't something you're going to let go of, so if you're asking for my help or support, I'll give you this: Let me consider it."

Carolyn nodded and pulled herself away from the crates, quickly dusting herself off before reaching her hand out toward Walsh. He stood as well and, after a brief hesitation, gave her a firm shake.

"Thank you," she said, looking him squarely in the eye. "If there's anything I have an understanding for, it's the value of giving your word. I sincerely appreciate your consideration, and I hope to work with you more on this. Your experience and history with this company are invaluable to me and to Phossium. I hope you know that you can come to me with anything."

Walsh held her eye contact and grasp in a classic seal-the-deal handshake and nodded. "You have my word, and I appreciate your honesty."

Carolyn didn't lose the smile she'd been holding back until well after she'd left Walsh's office. It was a difficult conversation, but she felt as though she'd made headway with someone who could truly help her make a difference at the organization . . . if she could, in fact, get him on board with turning Phossium's culture into one of peak performance.

One more chip at the mountain, she thought, and happily jogged the two flights of stairs back to her office.

CHAPTER 21

IT TAKES GUTS

ater that afternoon, Walsh heard a gentle tap on his door and immediately flicked off the turntable he kept next to his desk, cutting Billie Holiday off right in the middle of the bridge of "For Heaven's Sake."

"Yes?" he said gruffly, glancing up from the forms he'd been reviewing on his desk.

"Mr. Walsh?"

Batya was standing in the doorway, her report still in her hands.

"Come in, Batya," he said.

Batya wove her way into the room, carefully stepping around the stacks of files, folders, and miscellaneous electronics scattered around the floor, and waited until Walsh looked up from his work again. After a couple of minutes, he put down the forms and gave her a hard, questioning look.

Batya took the opening and launched right into it.

"Mr. Walsh, I'm not going to give you any more excuses about this report," she said, holding the sheaf of paper in front of her. "It's not up to my standards, and for that, I apologize. Apart from that, it's late, which I also apologize for. Since we spoke earlier, I've been updating it and plan to work on it the rest of this evening. You have my word that it will be on your desk, complete, by 9:00 a.m. tomorrow, and I will not allow such a breach of promise to happen again in the future."

Walsh waited for her to say more, but Batya seemed to have spoken her piece.

"Is that all?" he asked.

"It is," Batya said firmly.

Walsh nodded. "I see Carolyn got to you," he said, stating it almost like a question as he leaned back in his chair. Batya's brow furrowed.

"She didn't 'get to me,' Mr. Walsh," she said. "We had a good talk earlier, and what she had to say made sense. A lot of what she's trying to do here are things that I've been struggling with since I started at Phossium, and to be honest, I was considering quitting until she spoke with me today.

"We have a culture problem here, it's obvious," she continued. "But we can't sit around waiting for other people to fix it. It's on each of us to stand for what we believe and to get others to see how much better a place this can be—how much better we can work together—by taking action. I want to love what I do, and I want to do it well, but I can't do that until the people around me commit to doing their best, as well. So that's why I'm

here. I want you to know that I'm standing for something better, that I'm committed to keeping my word. And I hope that by doing so, it will make a difference with you and with those who work with us—and that it will eventually spread throughout the organization."

Batya's eyes never wavered from Walsh's as she spoke, the nervous edge that usually fringed her speech gone. Walsh was impressed, but he did his best not to show it.

"Are you saying that I don't keep my word?" he asked, testing her out of old habit.

Batya's eyes widened. "Oh no, not at all. That's not what I meant. I meant that I will be living by example from here on out, and I just want you to know that."

She shook her head. "We may have our differences, Mr. Walsh, but I've never known you to go against your word. That's one of the reasons I've stayed on as long as I have— you have integrity, and I respect that. And I'd like to work with more people who are like that. So, from here on out, I'm going to stand firmly for integrity, for standing by my word, and I'm going to encourage others to do the same."

> I WANT YOU TO KNOW THAT I'M STANDING FOR SOMETHING BETTER, **THAT I'M COMMITTED TO KEEPING MY WORD.**

Walsh nodded. It took a lot of guts for Batya to stand in front of him and say this, and because of that, he felt his respect for her grow just a little bit. And in the back of his mind, he also chalked up a few points for Carolyn. Despite his desire to stick with the status quo he'd been comfortable with for so many years, he was starting to see how there could, possibly, be room for improvement at Phossium.

With the hardest look he could muster, Walsh said, "I see. This doesn't change the fact that your report was late, but I appreciate you coming in here and acknowledging your responsibility in the matter, and I look forward to seeing the complete report first thing tomorrow."

Batya nodded firmly.

"Is there anything else?" he asked.

She shook her head. "No. Thank you for your time," she said, and made her way to the door.

Walsh gave a noncommittal grunt and turned back to his paperwork, listening as the door clicked shut and Batya's footsteps disappeared down the hallway. When he was certain she wasn't coming back, he let the vaguest smile flicker across his face.

Maybe it is time for a little bit of a change around here, he thought, *especially if that means working with people who care again.* It had been so long that he'd almost forgotten what that could be like.

CHAPTER 22
NEVER GIVE UP

The next week found Carolyn at her desk under a veritable mountain of paperwork. A note from Dolores had come in that morning, requesting updated financial reports from every department, and that along with her ever-growing to-do list and regular work had her head swimming.

At this rate, I won't be caught up until the middle of next year . . . if then, she thought.

It was early afternoon when a soft knock at the door jolted her out of her workflow.

"Come in," she said without looking up. She heard the shuffle of feet as whoever it was made their way to her desk, then a soft cough followed by, "Is this a bad time?"

Carolyn looked up from the glow of her screen and jumped. Standing in front of her were Walsh and Batya, and Batya, bless her, was holding out a fresh cup of coffee from the café just down the street.

"Batya, you are amazing, thank you," she said, taking the cup and enjoying a grateful sip. Batya smiled while Walsh glowered impatiently. With her free hand, Carolyn gestured to the guest chairs.

"Please, sit down," she said, and as they both settled into their seats, she continued, "I have to say, I'm really surprised to see both of you here. What's up?"

Batya looked at Walsh, who looked at her as though waiting for her to talk, so she did.

"Well, after you and I spoke last week, I spoke briefly with Mr. Walsh and acknowledged the breach I'd made when I was late with that report. I told him I'd turn it in the next day, which I did, and kind of left it at that. This morning, however, we ran into each other in the break room, and he started asking me some questions about integrity and culture, and I thought it would be best if we both came and spoke with you." She looked over at Walsh, who nodded in agreement.

Carolyn raised her eyebrows over the rim of her coffee cup.

"That's great," she said, setting the coffee down. "I'm so glad you talked, and Batya, thank you for being intentional about standing by your word."

Batya nodded and smiled.

"So, what questions do you have?" she asked.

Batya looked at Walsh again, and this time he took the lead.

"I'm still weighing the merits of this whole 'culture' concept, but Batya's acknowledgement last week was . . . welcome."

Carolyn smiled and almost thanked him out loud when Walsh suddenly held up his hand.

"That doesn't mean I'm supporting you and these changes you're trying to make," said Walsh, "not by any means, but if you do persist in this, how exactly do you plan to make it happen?"

Carolyn nodded. "I appreciate the healthy skepticism, Hugh. And I'm glad you got to see what we're trying to do in action with Batya. Standing by your word—having integrity and acknowledging when you breach that trust—I believe are vital to a peak-performing culture. But we also have to be intentional about it. We have to be conscious of the fact that we give our word several times a day, if not dozens of times, and we need to stand by that word every time we give it, so being aware of our integrity is key.

"The other big part is persistence," Carolyn continued. "We can have integrity, and we can be intentional about giving our word and standing by it, but we also need to know that standing by

our word means doing it no matter what and always, not just for now, but from now on."

Carolyn looked at Walsh and Batya, who nodded, although both still had questioning looks on their faces.

"Let me explain what I mean by 'persist,'" she said. "Persistence is the lynchpin of cultural transformation. We could decide to have integrity and intentionality in our words and actions, but if we just stopped one day and let our promises slip by unfulfilled, then everything we've done before then becomes pointless.

"A couple of weeks ago, for instance, I met with one of the department heads . . . doesn't matter which one," she said with a dismissive wave. There was no point in calling anyone out. "I asked this person for a report, and it was turned in . . . only it was several days late. However, I didn't question it at all. I just said 'thank you' and went on with what I was doing."

"Looking back on that incident, it occurred to me that I never trusted the report would be turned in on time in the first place. In fact, I'd given a deadline of one full week before I needed it just to account for the inevitable delay. That is not acceptable. I shouldn't have to organize my work schedule around other people's lack of integrity, and I shouldn't have to prod people to get their work done on time. Our efforts—at work just as much as in life—should simply be the best we can do at that time, every time."

PERSISTENCE IS THE LYNCHPIN OF
CULTURAL TRANSFORMATION.

"But by allowing that report to be late, you'd kind of given your permission for that default culture to continue . . . right?" said Batya.

Carolyn nodded. "Absolutely. Everything we do has a ripple effect. In allowing reports to be late, I let people think that deadlines don't matter. And those people probably let their teams think the same thing. So, the cycle continues, on and on," she said. "Because we've accepted this mentality, we've created a default culture that we now have to pull ourselves out of, and, to do that, we need to be unwavering in our commitment to something better, and, frankly, we have to be loud about it.

"We're not only going to stand for intentional integrity with unflappable persistence, but we also need to let everyone know, in clear terms, that we are going to give them our absolute best from here on out—and that we expect the very same from everyone else," she said. "We can't give up."

Walsh nodded and shifted forward a little in his chair, tugging down at the hem of his sweater as he said, "I see what you're saying, about the ripple effect and all, but I don't see how beating other team members over the head with how 'great' we are and how 'trustworthy' we can be, and then shaming them for not being that way, is going to work. Seems like just another way to cause divides."

Carolyn nodded enthusiastically. "Exactly! And I'm so glad you brought that up. It was something I was thinking about last night, and if I wasn't a mother, I might not have been able to give you a clear answer to that . . . or at least, it would have taken me a lot longer to figure out."

CHAPTER 23
FEEDBACK

Carolyn turned the seaside picture of her family on her desk toward Batya and Walsh and pointed at her daughter.

"Sadie, believe it or not, was my biggest challenge out of the two kids. She was as stubborn as they get and often chose to do what she wanted to do instead of what I or her father or her teachers told her to do. It got her in a lot of trouble, and for a while there, I had no idea how to handle it. But then a good friend of mine, in a very kind way, suggested that I try changing my approach to discipline. Instead of saying something like, 'Why are you always so stubborn?' I could try reminding her first that I knew she was a good person, and she was better than that behavior."

Carolyn got up, walked over to Batya, and said, "Imagine if you turned in a report to me two days late, or a report that was only half done, and I said, 'Batya, this is awful. You're a disgrace to this company.'

"Or worse," Carolyn continued, walking over to Walsh, "what if I just let it slide, but I said to Hugh later on, 'Hugh, can you believe that Batya? She does terrible work, if she does it at all, and it's always late. I can't believe we still keep her around, blah, blah, blah . . . .'"

"All I've done is made you, Batya, feel bad, and if I gossiped to Hugh about you, I've also made you look bad in front of him. And if he's also a gossip, I've made you look bad in front of the whole company. Not a good morale booster, right?" said Carolyn.

"Right," said Batya.

"Instead, what if I received your report—late, incomplete, whatever the case was—and instead of shaming you, I said, 'Batya, I need to share something with you, and my motive is for you to be a relevant and powerful part of our team. You know integrity is a shared value in our group, and lately you have not been sharing in that value. Your work was late. It was underprepared. But Batya, I refuse to tolerate anything other than you being your best self—and you're so much better than this. There are endless possibilities in front of you, if people feel that they can trust and depend on you—but that only happens when you are seen as trustworthy, which only happens when you honor your word as your life. Do you understand that I'm sharing this with you because I genuinely care about you and want you to be the best you can possibly be?'"

Batya blinked and nodded. "That makes all the difference. If you tell me you believe in me, that you believe I'm better than what I've done, then I *want* to be better. I want to be the person you think I am . . . that *I* think I am."

Carolyn smiled.

"Exactly," she said, and then looked over at Walsh. "And what do you think? Is that a reasonable approach?"

Walsh had a studious look on his face. "That makes sense, and it's not coddling, which was how I thought you were going to answer. I can see how that would help."

He nodded to Carolyn and Batya and stood up.

"Thank you for talking through that," he said, shaking Carolyn's hand. "I'll take it into consideration. In the meantime . . . I wouldn't

mind if more of my team members took the same approach to responsibility and integrity as Batya has."

Batya grinned. "I plan to help them get there," she said, standing with Walsh, who also gave her a strong handshake. "Thank you for taking the time to listen, Mr. Walsh."

Walsh nodded and, without another word, turned and walked out of the room. Batya and Carolyn watched him go, and then Batya turned to Carolyn. "I was so surprised when he asked me about all this, and even more surprised when he agreed to come up and see you," she said. "And I'm glad he did, because I learned even more today."

Carolyn smiled, nodded with a quick "happy to," and began to walk back behind her desk when Batya suddenly said, "But Mr. Walsh wasn't the only reason I came up here, Mrs. Qualey. I wanted to introduce you to someone. Do you have a minute?"

Carolyn gave the stack of paper and fifteen open windows on her laptop a despairing look, but said, "Of course." Until she felt confident that she had a firm foundation for this better culture to grow on, establishing that foundation was her top priority.

"Great," said Batya. "Follow me."

HONOR YOUR WORD AS YOUR LIFE.

CHAPTER 24

FOUNDATION OF A PEAK PERFORMANCE CULTURE

Carolyn and Batya walked downstairs to document processing, and as they entered the hallway, they suddenly heard a burst of group laughter coming from the door that Carolyn had almost knocked on ages ago when she'd first visited the main DP department with her legacy-letter copy request. She was shocked at herself for not coming by since then, and it was this door that Batya walked up to and swung open with a preemptory knock.

"Hey guys," she said as she walked in. "I hope we're not interrupting."

"Not at all," someone said.

"Come on in!" added another.

As Carolyn walked in, she was surprised to see a group of about seven document-processing assistants, all of whom smiled at her and waved. It wasn't just the smiles that surprised her, however—it was the room. Instead of the typical arrangement of desks-to-walls with low dividers, as the main DP room was arranged, the group had set up their desks in the center of the room, three to a side, with one young man's desk capping the end.

"Hi," she said.

"I think you all remember Mrs. Qualey, our new CEO," said Batya.

Everyone nodded, and Carolyn smiled back at each of them.

"I remember meeting your team a couple of weeks after I started," she said, recalling the brief introductory meeting she'd held with

the entire DP department as part of her orientation. "It's good to see you all in such fine spirits. What's the occasion?"

"We were just celebrating a milestone," said the young man sitting at the cap-desk. As he stood to greet her, Carolyn found herself somewhat surprised by how handsomely he was dressed, from the vibrant blue and white floral pattern oxford to the perfectly matched pair of suede dress shoes and light gray suit. His dark eyes shone with merriment as he explained, "One hundred thousandth document in the Codsworth file scanned!"

A couple of soft cheers rippled through the room again, and for the first time, Carolyn noticed the walls. A hand-drawn thermometer labeled "Codsworth" with the number "150,432" at the top was freshly colored in up to the 100,000 mark. Other thermometers were at various stages of completion, and another wall labeled "Victory!" had dozens of topped-off thermometers taped below it.

WE NEED TO STAND IN THE PATH OF THIS DEFAULT CULTURE AND SAY **WE WILL NOT BUDGE IN OUR COMMITMENT TO INTEGRITY.**

"This is amazing," said Carolyn, gesturing toward the colorful display. "Who came up with this?"

No one answered for a moment, and then a young woman spoke up.

"Raj did," she said, nodding toward the man standing next to her.

Raj shook his head in embarrassment.

"We all did, Joyce," he said.

"Well, it was your idea," said Joyce with a smile. To Carolyn she said, "He comes up with all of our initiatives. We have a 'thank-you' wall over there, too, for when we want to give a shout-out to our teammates for helping out, and a 'penalty jar' for when we miss a goal number by a certain date. Whenever we complete a thermometer, we have a pizza party and use the penalty jar to pay for some of it . . . though there hasn't been a lot in there recently. And Raj makes sure we get that party every single time."

"Thank you, Joyce," said Raj with a playfully embarrassed smile. Then to Carolyn he said, "She gives me too much credit. We all came up with these ideas, and we all pitch in on the parties. I mean, it's a lot of work, and these numbers are worth celebrating!"

There was a short burst of laughter and applause from the room, and Carolyn nodded in agreement.

"They certainly are," she said. "You have all done an excellent job, and I love the direction you're going with this! Keep it up. And from now on, the pizza parties are on me."

There was a tumult of applause at the announcement.

"You deserve it!" she said, smiling. Then she looked at Raj. "Raj, do you have some time to talk?" she asked. "It shouldn't take long, maybe about an hour or so."

Raj looked surprised. "Of course," he said, glancing down at his calendar. "I don't have anything on the books for the rest of the day—just good ol' fashioned paperwork."

"Come with us," she said, and to the room she added, "Keep up the great work!"

"Thanks guys," said Batya, waving to everyone once more before following Carolyn and Raj out.

Carolyn and Batya walked with Raj up to the CEO office, where Carolyn offered them both a seat and then took her preferred stance of leaning casually against the front of her desk. She smiled at Raj, who gave her a curious grin.

"Sorry for springing this on you out of the blue, Raj . . . may I call you Raj?" Carolyn asked, realizing she was using the nickname his team members used for him.

"Oh, of course. I don't think I would answer to anything else. Certainly not 'Rajan,' unless you're my mom . . . or my wife," he said with a short laugh, and then added, "and I'm more than happy to meet with you. I mean, I don't know what this is about, but it feels like it might be important," he said, looking back and forth at both Carolyn and Batya.

"It is," they replied at the same time, then laughed at each other. Batya shook her head in embarrassment. "I'm sorry, Mrs. Qualey. I guess I'm just excited to get this going . . . and for Raj to hear about it. I think he's going to be one of your biggest supporters."

"Not at all, Batya. I love the enthusiasm," Carolyn replied, and then turned to Raj. "What I wanted to talk with you about is 'culture.' In the few months I've been here, I've learned that most of this company is simply getting by with a culture that's in default mode. No one seems to be standing for anything more than the status quo . . . except for a few people, including yourself and your team and Batya here."

For the next half hour, Carolyn, with the help of Batya, explained as much as they could about default culture, integrity, intentionality, and persistence, from the discovery and meaning behind "The Match in the Root Cellar" story to Carolyn's reasoning behind the foundations for creating a true peak performance culture. Raj asked questions here and there, but, as he explained to them, this company-wide approach to creating a peak-performing culture sounded like what he and his team had been trying to live by, just on a much larger and more defined scale.

"Your team is an amazing example of standing up for something better, even in the midst of such a poor default culture," Carolyn said to Raj after he shared his own team's seemingly natural desire for honesty and trust. "What you're doing is what everyone in this company should be doing. We should be collaborating, we should be supporting each other and holding each other accountable, and we should be standing by our word, even if it's something as simple as saying we'll hold a pizza party for hitting a goal no matter what.

"But it's not something we can do alone," said Carolyn. "We can be intentional about having integrity, and we can persist in those things no matter what, but one match—or even three matches—doesn't light up a whole room. We need more matches, we need more light . . . like your team, Raj.

"This is our challenge," she continued. "I need both of you to speak with Raj's team and explain what we're going for. Tell them about the difference between a default culture and a peak-performing one, and the vital necessity of building this foundation of integrity, intentionality, and persistence. Then we need to start getting others on board. We not only need team members beyond this group to desire integrity in themselves and others, but we also need everyone in our organization to see that this is something that affects every last one of us."

"Of course," said Raj. "I'll speak with my team about it today. But, Mrs. Qualey, I don't think we're the only people in the company who will be willing to back this and spread it to others. I can think of at least six or seven other people in other departments who would be just as happy to get this wildfire going."

Carolyn nodded, the excitement building in her. "In that case, I think we need to go ahead and set up a meeting. Can the two of you identify as many potential 'early adopters' as you can from around the company? It doesn't matter what department they're in. I want everyone we can get, and the more people there, the better."

By now, Carolyn was pacing the room. "Every day in this default culture is hurting us and driving this company toward failure. The simple fact is that we should all desire nothing less than the best for each other and for our customers, but unless we can understand and embrace that, and soon, this whole business is in danger."

She stopped and looked at both of them, holding their gaze long enough so that they understood the importance of what she was saying.

"We cannot waiver on this," she said. "We cannot demand any less than this. We need to stand in the path of this default culture and say we will not budge in our commitment to integrity. Frankly, we need to have a type of bravery that is hard to come by in this world; we need to have the courage to stand, incessantly and persistently, for what we believe."

She stopped, and the excited looks on their faces filled her with joy.

"What do you think, team? Are you up for this?"

"Absolutely!" said Batya, grinning.

"We're all in," Raj added, his smile just as strong and genuine.

"Then let's make this happen," said Carolyn.

CHAPTER 25

THE GATHERING

It took about two weeks to set everything up, to get the right candidates on board, and for Carolyn to do more research and put the final details on her presentation. There was a lot more to it than she'd expected, but each part was essential.

On the day of the big meeting, Carolyn walked in the room to find it filled with dozens of bright faces. Some she recognized from different departments, a junior marketing assistant here and a senior coordinator over there, and even a couple of the mail clerks whom she'd come to know by name. Others, she was sad to realize, were people she'd either never met before or whom she vaguely recognized but couldn't put a name to. *That's another thing that's definitely going to change*, she determined. *Once this new culture is rolling, we'll all be on a first-name basis.*

At the front of the room were Batya, Raj, and Raj's entire team, every one of them smiling broadly. Carolyn smiled and waved to them, and as she did, the whole team erupted into applause, followed quickly by the rest of the room.

Carolyn did her best to say "Thank you" over the din of the room. Just as she turned to walk to the front of the room, however, she saw someone else already standing at the podium, and his hard stare stopped her dead in her tracks.

The room grew quiet as Carolyn debated over what to do. *What's he going to say?* she wondered. Was this it? Was it all over before it even began? Sudden images of Dolores grasping her arms in fake condolence and saying, "I'm sorry, but we just have to let you go," began running through her head. Throwing caution to the wind, she began to walk with steely resolve toward the podium, determined to steamroll over any protests the large man might put up, when something else stopped her again.

It was the first smile she'd ever seen Hugh Walsh give, and it instantly shed fifteen years off his face. He gestured her to join him at the podium, the bewildered look on her face causing him to smile just a little more.

Once she was standing next to him, Walsh began.

"Most of you here today know me, and if you don't, you will. My name is Hugh Walsh, customer relations manager, and I don't think any of you, Mrs. Qualey included, are as surprised to see me standing here as I am.

"If you'd asked me a month ago what I thought of our new CEO, I wouldn't have given you a very polite answer. It's not her fault that old Oz, the former CEO, retired, but Oz and I, as some of you remember, went way back. He had a leadership style that was sometimes eccentric, but we were used to it.

"Then before we knew it, our company was bought up, and this spunky little upstart comes in and starts turning everything on its head," he said, thrusting a stubby thumb in Carolyn's direction and looking at her sternly, though his eyes were smiling.

"From day one, she was putting her nose in everyone's business. I tell you, I got more complaints from the staff around here in those first few months than I'd gotten in the last four years combined.

"But what they were complaining about was interesting. It wasn't annoyance over any kind of unnecessary roadblocks she was putting up or anger at her attitude or anything like that. It was frustration, because she was forcing them to work differently. Not that they weren't working before, of course, but what she was doing was driving them to work together, to communicate with other departments and adopt new methods that, God forbid, might improve our efficiency and overall connectivity—with each other and with customers.

"But then she managed to do something that really pissed me off. She walked in on the middle of a departmental reprimand and walked away with that team member without so much as an explanation," he said.

"I have to say I was pretty upset about the whole ordeal, but that same day, only a few hours later, she came back and not only openly apologized, but she also told me something that rang true . . . and I respected her for it, though it was hard to hear at the time.

"What she told me had to do with integrity and the unfortunate lack of it at Phossium. Now, for someone like me, who practically grew up here, to hear that from some newbie CEO was not easy. I didn't care to hear what she said, and I didn't care to agree, but I've come to believe that she has a point . . . and a pretty good one at that. And I've been impressed as hell by the team members that are already taking up this attitude and sparking the foundation for a real, trustworthy, integrity-driven culture.

"But you didn't come here to hear from me, so, first of all, thank you for your patience, and, second, let me introduce you to your fire starter, your CEO, Mrs. Carolyn Qualey."

Carolyn fought the sudden swelling of emotion in her chest, firmly shook Walsh's hand, and thanked him. He smiled and gave her a solid handshake in return.

"Hope you can follow that up," he said with an unexpected wink and then turned around and took his place next to Batya in the front row.

Carolyn's heart felt close to bursting as she looked around. She couldn't help feeling an overwhelming sense of joy and pride layering over her shock and appreciation for Walsh's introduction. As much as she'd felt like a failure over the past few months, this gathering, this phenomenal and thoroughly unexpected reception, made everything worth it.

This is where it starts, she thought. *These are the people who are going to make this happen, and I couldn't be prouder of them.*

"Thank you, Hugh, for such a kind and honest introduction," she said, giving him a smile as he nodded in acknowledgement. "And thank you, all of you, for being here today. Change in any form is not easy, and the fact that you're willing to hear what I have to say speaks volumes to your character.

"And now for the serious part. First and foremost, I want all of you to understand that none of what I'm about to tell you can happen if you and everyone else in this organization aren't committed to change," she said.

There was a murmur of affirmation from the room.

"I'm going to hold you accountable for it, just as I expect you to hold me accountable in return. We're in this together," Carolyn said. "And just as importantly, I want you all to understand that this is not something that's happening because I'm the 'boss' and in a position of power. That has nothing to do with it. Any one of you could have done this before me, and every one of you will be actively making it happen after this day is over. Any one person can *activate* a better culture, but no one person can make it happen alone."

ANY ONE PERSON CAN ACTIVATE A BETTER CULTURE, BUT **NO ONE PERSON CAN MAKE IT HAPPEN ALONE.**

She glanced down at her notes briefly and smiled. "If I'd had a book on this, I'd have given it to you to read instead of dragging you into a presentation. Maybe that's the next step," she said. "But for now, we'll do this in the 'new' old-school style."

She turned to the large screen set several feet back from the podium and flipped to the first slide. The screen glowed with the word "culture."

CHAPTER 26

LAYING THE FOUNDATION

"**B**efore going any further, I want to make sure we're all on the same page about what the word 'culture' means," said Carolyn. "Culture is the line that separates the behaviors that a group will tolerate, and even advocate for, from those behaviors that the group will not.

"Whether it's two people or a whole organization, a group draws this culture line, and most of the time, they're not even aware that they're doing it. It just happens—and a 'default' culture is created, and if that culture isn't addressed, it can lead to poor communication, poor productivity, and, in the case of an organization, its eventual closure.

"The good news is that we don't *have* to accept it! Instead, we can intentionally shape our culture into one that encourages all of us to dare noble, bold, and mighty things—and achieve them. We can have a culture that drives peak performance if we actively advocate for it and shun anything less.

"And central to that peak performance culture is integrity."

The screen behind her flickered, and a new slide appeared.

"Having integrity means doing what you say you're going to do. That's it. It's not a moral statement, it's not right or wrong; it's simply a condition.

"A smartphone, for instance, has integrity when each individual part does what it's supposed to do, interacts with the other parts exactly as it's supposed to, and allows you to access an app, hop on the Internet, send a text, or just make a call. The intention behind how it's used can be moralistic, but in and of itself, a smartphone is without intention; it is agnostic.

"Our organization, as any other, consists of individual parts. It's when those parts are doing as they're expected to—when the parts can rely on each other to keep their word and perform the functions needed—that organizations achieve optimal output: their peak performance. And the intention we put behind these actions is what we use our peak-performing culture to achieve.

"So how do we do this?

"First, we need to understand that shaping and living a peak performance culture is not something we can create and then just walk away from. It needs to be generated every hour of every day."

Carolyn clicked to the next slide.

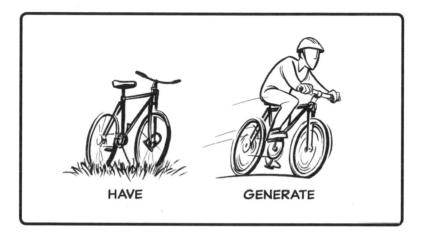

"In other words," she continued, "culture is not something we can fix—just like being fit or having a loving relationship is not something we can just turn on and it stays that way effortlessly. It is not a problem to be solved but a challenge to be managed, and managing it—just like being fit, just like with a loving relationship—is something you have to *persist* in doing."

She looked behind her as the next image appeared, boldly centering on the word "trust."

"When we're persistent about doing what we say we're going to do," she continued, "we become trustworthy, and trustworthiness is an essential characteristic of any one person or group that chooses to lead. It's required for authenticity, for vulnerability, for intimacy; and it's the seed of a peak performance culture."

She stopped then and looked at the audience. Dozens of curious eyes met her gaze, and after a moment, she pushed herself slightly on tiptoe and turned her gaze to the back of the room.

"Jeff," she said, indicating the dark-haired young man who ran the front desk.

"Yes, ma'am?" he said.

"When was the last time you told someone you would be there in 'just a second?'" she asked.

Jeff looked perplexed. "I don't know, maybe this morning? It's like, just a throwaway line, right? You don't really remember when you use it because you use it all the time."

Carolyn nodded. "You're absolutely right; it is a line we all use all of the time. But if we're choosing to live with integrity, then if we speak that line and we're *not* there in a second, then we've lied to someone. We've lost trust, and we've lost integrity."

She flipped to the next screen.

WISDOM IS THE CORRECT NAMING OF THINGS.

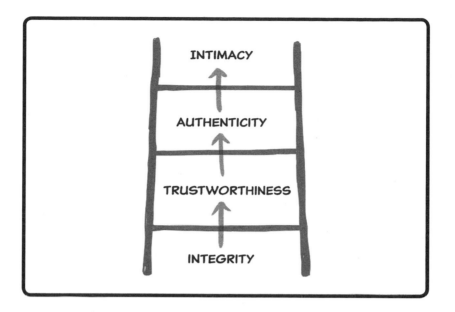

"Why do we lie so often?" she asked, as three statements popped up on the slide.

Just a second.

I'll be there in a minute.

I'll be home at 5:00 p.m.

She pointed to each line as she said, "Rarely is it just a second, just a minute, or at 5:00 p.m. when you walk in the door.

"We give our word with such disregard. We schedule back-to-back meetings in different locations or develop annual goals and never follow through with them. We tell coworkers we'll have a report ready at noon on Wednesday, but then we don't, because 'something came up.'"

Three more statements materialized on the screen.

I'll get back to you on this.

Let's have coffee.

I'm going to look into that.

"In every case we give our word, but we're not being intentional about it. We're not staying aware of the fact that *with this phrase, I just made a promise to someone*. It's like Jeff said: We think of it as a throwaway. But it shouldn't be—none of these should be, because here's the thing . . . ." said Carolyn, and all six statements behind her faded into one short phrase, bright white against a solid black background:

ALL WE HAVE IS OUR WORD.

She turned around and looked at her audience again.

"So, what do *you* have?" she asked.

She let the question hang in the air for a moment, then added, "Imagine what it would be like to live in a place where you could depend on those around you to do what they say they're going to do 100 percent of the time. Status meetings would no longer be necessary. Complex projects involving multiple people and interdependencies would be completed on time. Synchronicity would skyrocket.

"In essence, the possibilities for achievement would be limitless."

CHAPTER 27

AVOIDING "THE TRAP"

arolyn took questions for almost half an hour after her presentation, stressing repeatedly the value of integrity and the importance of being both intentional about it and persistent in it. She explained the importance of acknowledging breaches of integrity as well, sharing with them the same feedback method she'd explained to Batya and Walsh a couple of weeks before.

Afterward, she was once again humbled by the applause and shook as many hands as she could on the way out, thanking each of them for being there and for being a light in this new culture. She was also pleasantly surprised to see a few members of her remaining leadership team, who stopped to thank her both for the presentation as well as for demonstrating integrity and proper feedback to them early on.

She shook her head. "I still kick myself for blowing up that day, but I'm glad we were able to repair the breach. Thank you for accepting it and for your willingness to be a part of this."

She left the meeting with a thousand thoughts running through her mind. The seeds had been planted, but she needed early-adopters out there who actively stood for intentional integrity, provided the right kind of feedback, and guided others on how to acknowledge breaches when they happened. She knew she could count on Batya, Raj, and most, if not all, of Raj's team. And Walsh . . . .

> THE SEEDS HAD BEEN PLANTED, BUT SHE NEEDED EARLY-ADOPTERS OUT THERE WHO ACTIVELY STOOD FOR INTENTIONAL INTEGRITY, PROVIDED THE RIGHT KIND OF FEEDBACK, AND **GUIDED OTHERS ON HOW TO ACKNOWLEDGE BREACHES WHEN THEY HAPPENED.**

She still couldn't get over Hugh Walsh. He'd been like a brick wall since the day she met him, impossible to move, though he'd shown some interest in the past couple of weeks. He wasn't the first person she saw joining her in supporting a peak performance culture by a long shot, but to hear that speech he gave—she was still grinning when she opened the door to her office . . .

. . . and promptly walked into an ice storm.

CHAPTER 28

YOU'RE DONE HERE

Dolores looked up from Carolyn's desk as Carolyn came to a sudden stop in her doorway. As always, Dolores was coldly elegant as she sat there, her hands folded over the ubiquitous tablet.

Surprised for a moment, all Carolyn could think of was how dumpy she felt compared to Dolores. If she spent three hours every day getting ready, she thought, she still wouldn't manage to look as put-together as Dolores probably did when she first rolled out of bed in the morning.

As she stood there, Dolores rose from Carolyn's chair and walked around the desk, a muddled look of concern and disappointment creasing her carefully made face.

"Big meeting today?" she asked, tapping the tablet nonchalantly against her palm.

"Yes, there was," said Carolyn, confused. "Is there something wrong? It was an internal meeting, so I didn't think to invite to you, but if you'd like me to recap. . . ."

"No, that's quite alright," Dolores said, cutting her off. "Unless that meeting had to do with that list I gave you. But it didn't, did it? Nor did it have anything to do with the expenses that continue to bleed this company out daily. In fact, it had nothing to do with anything we talked about last month, did it?"

She stopped in front of Carolyn and shook her head.

"I tried to give you the benefit of the doubt, Carolyn, but I can only be so lenient for so long. You're in a powerful position, and I needed you to use that power to turn the financial tide of this company quickly and efficiently. For some reason, however, you've refused to accept this and have made this little 'mission' of yours a top priority," she sighed. "Why can't you understand that this isn't about people? It's not about Oz and his whatever-you-called-it, 'Founder's Mentality.' It's not about the working environment, and right now, it's not about the customer. It's about getting our numbers straight before we can even think about rebuilding ourselves in the marketplace."

Dolores reached out and put a conciliatory hand on Carolyn's arm. "I'm afraid I've let you go about this all wrong for too long in the hopes you would come to your senses, but enough is enough. I have to let you go."

Carolyn felt the blood rush from her face. Had it really been four weeks since she and Dolores last spoke? Was it a coincidence that she showed up on the same day as the big meeting, or had someone told her about it? Not that it mattered, of course. In fact, Carolyn now wished Dolores had been able to attend, but that was neither here nor there. A thousand thoughts were racing through her mind, but before she could voice one of them, Dolores turned away from her, cast

a glance around the room, and said, "Of course, I'll have to step in for a little bit, just to get things back on track. It will be difficult to balance running this company with my other duties, but at least we'll have someone running this organization who has its best interests in mind."

THIS COMPANY HAS TO BE REBUILT FROM THE INSIDE-OUT, AND IF YOU TOOK A MOMENT TO LOOK AROUND, DOLORES, YOU'D SEE THAT INCREDIBLE CHANGE IS ALREADY WORKING ITS WAY IN.

With that last thinly veiled insult, Carolyn finally regained her voice.

"You know, for someone with such good taste, you certainly seem to have very narrow vision," said Carolyn, fire burning in her eyes. "When Algus approached me about taking on Phossium, I was excited, but I also knew it wasn't going to be a quick or easy process. Phossium has good bones, and at one point it had a good reputation; but time and neglect have turned it into a shadow of itself, a monument to quality now worn, broken, and half buried in the sand. To repair this will take far more than spit and elbow grease, and it will take far more than a few months. This company has to be rebuilt from the inside-out, and if you took a moment to look around, Dolores, you'd see that incredible change is already working its way in."

Dolores's eyes narrowed. "The only change I see is the one that's about to happen right now: You're done, Carolyn. Take your little book collection and secondhand chairs and coddling attitude and get out of my building."

With that, Dolores turned sharply, scooped her bag off the guest chair, and flung open the office door . . .

. . . only to be stopped cold.

Standing in the doorway were Hugh Walsh and Bertrand Wagner, the head of Algus's board of directors. Both looked startled at Dolores's sudden appearance, but not nearly as startled as Dolores herself. She managed to stop just short of ramming into them, pedaling ungracefully a couple of steps back into the office as she quickly composed herself.

"Why, Bert, what a surprise!" she said, forcing a smile on her face so fast that Carolyn could have sworn she heard it break the sound barrier.

"Ms. Pendergrast," Wagner nodded. "It's good to see both of you. Looks like you're keeping an excellent eye on our chief, here," he said with a smile.

"It's good to see you both, as well," Carolyn said, smiling, as she shook Wagner's and Walsh's hands and forced down the hurricane of emotions rolling within her. "Please, come in. Have a seat."

Walsh followed Wagner into the room, but both remained standing. Walsh's eyes were cold and hard as he looked at Dolores.

"Thank you, Mrs. Qualey, but I'm not staying long," said Wagner. "I was in the area and realized I haven't seen you since your first day here, so I thought I'd drop by and personally invite you to our quarterly board meeting next month. On the way, however, I was waylaid by Hugh here," he said, gesturing toward Walsh.

Walsh nodded but kept his stern gaze focused on Dolores. Dolores's composure flickered as a wave of concern rippled over her, but it was gone as quickly as it appeared.

Wagner apparently hadn't noticed the exchange.

"What he had to say was very interesting," he said, still speaking to Carolyn. "It sounds like you have some fascinating plans for this place, which I understand have to do with this focus on company culture and the importance of integrity. Now, I've known Hugh here since Phossium's glory days—we used to be one of their best customers until this acquisition became possible—and he's not an easy man to impress, but somehow you've managed to earn some serious points with him, Mrs. Qualey."

Carolyn felt herself blushing, but held Wagner's gaze and nodded appreciatively. "I'm flattered, truly. Mr. Walsh has been an invaluable source of company knowledge and support, and it means a lot to me that he would reach out to you," Carolyn said.

Wagner nodded and, with a quick look over at Dolores, said, "Mrs. Qualey, I know that we're still working to bring up the numbers here, but after speaking with Hugh, it looks like you're on the right track to make that happen. I'd appreciate it if you'd speak to this approach you're taking to culture at our meeting, as well as share the impacts it's had on the staff and, hopefully by then, on our bottom line."

He reached out and Carolyn shook his hand firmly in confirmation. "I'd be honored, Mr. Wagner," she said. "And by next month, I believe we'll have some more impressive figures to share with you and the board, as well."

Wagner placed his other hand over hers and smiled. "I have no doubt, Mrs. Qualey. Thank you." With that, he glanced down at his wristwatch and raised an eyebrow. "Looks like I have to run if I'm going to make it to my next meeting," he said, turning to Dolores. "Ms. Pendergrast, thank you for being so attentive to Mrs. Qualey here—it appears she's really starting to make a difference with this place, and I'm sure you've been a valuable part of that. I do hope you'll be at the meeting as well?"

Dolores nodded. "She's impressed me from the start, Bert. I will certainly be at the meeting, and I look forward to Mrs. Qualey's presentation. You're such a dear for stopping by."

Wagner gave her a brief smile, and Dolores quickly added, "Do let me know if you'll be out this way again. I would love to take you to lunch!"

Wagner nodded politely and continued out the door while Walsh gave Carolyn a quick, indecipherable look and followed him out.

An awkward silence filled the room as the two women stood there, neither one moving. Finally, Carolyn broke the silence.

"Looks like my secondhand chairs will be here a while longer," she said, looking over at Dolores with a soft smile.

Dolores glared at her. "That was luck," she said. "And now, I won't have to go through the ordeal of explaining to the board why we had to let you go. You'll show them all by yourself at the meeting." She arched a cold eyebrow at her. "I'm looking forward to hearing what you'll have to say."

And with that, she left.

Carolyn remained standing for a moment, long enough to be sure Dolores was gone, and then collapsed into one of the guest chairs, flinging both arms out and taking deep, long breaths as she stared at the ceiling. After a minute, she raised her arms and pressed both hands to her face.

My God, *what a day,* she thought, and then glanced at the small silver wristwatch she always wore: 12:30 p.m. *And we're only getting started,* she thought with a sigh. She let herself stay in the chair for a few more minutes and then pulled herself up, brushed herself off, ran a hand through the soft waves of her hair, and took a deep, calming, restorative breath.

Now for that bottom line, she thought.

CHAPTER 29

WARNING BELLS

The encounter with Dolores—and Wagner and Walsh—was still washing over Carolyn as she worked her way through the 501 CEO duties she needed to get to that day, so it wasn't until a little after six when she finally got a chance to take a break and clear her head. She quickly changed into a pair of jeans she kept at the office, laced on some sneakers, pulled her hair into a loose ponytail, and took off for a quick walk along the trail that looped through the back of Phossium's property.

It was only a few steps to the stairwell, but just as she turned the corner, she was stopped in her tracks by an enormous desk wedged in the entryway. She poked her head into the stairwell above the desk and glanced down. Office furniture was in various stages of ascent, a convoy of movers in matching green-and-brown uniforms hauling the various pieces around the sharp curves of the stairs.

Suddenly, she heard a grunt followed by a gruff "excuse us" and noticed two movers standing at the other end of the stair-blocking desk. He and his partner had been taking a break before maneuvering the desk into the hallway.

She couldn't believe she'd forgotten about the move, but today was the day they'd scheduled Raj's team to move into the larger office space down the hall from her office. Over the coming weeks, she planned to bring at least twice as many team members as he had now into his department, and she wanted Raj to feel comfortable with creating the same kind of team-building atmosphere that he'd so adeptly put together in his current space.

She quickly apologized to the movers and turned to take the stairs at the other end when she remembered that one was also off limits—closed for painting for the week.

Reluctantly, she called the elevator, regretting the opportunity to work off some excess energy on the four flights down. A moment later the doors slid open, and Carolyn met the surprised look of a young man in a worn corduroy jacket with a bundle of file folders clasped under one arm.

"Mrs. Qualey?" he asked.

"Yes?" she said.

"Oh good, I'm glad I caught you," he said, stepping out of the elevator. "I was afraid you'd left for the day."

Carolyn smiled. "Some days I wish I had those kind of office hours," she said. "Rest assured, you can catch me in my office at this time just about any day."

He smiled. "I believe it," he said, then quickly shot out his hand. "I should introduce myself. My name is Josh Templeton. I work

I'M PRETTY SURE I COULD LOSE MY JOB BY TALKING WITH YOU ABOUT THIS.

in customer relations. We met briefly when you came through the department a few months back."

She shook his hand. "Of course, Josh. I recognize you, though thank you for reminding me of your name. Unfortunately, I'm still learning everyone's name."

"No problem," he said, and then started to say something when he suddenly seemed to notice her shoes. "Oh, no, you were headed out, weren't you?"

Carolyn shook her head and laughed a little. "Not really. I was just going to take a walk on that trail that runs next to the property line and get a little fresh air. Would you like to join me?"

Josh smiled. "Actually, that sounds great. Mind if I . . . ?" he held up the files under his arm, and Carolyn quickly nodded.

"Of course. Just drop them anywhere in my office," she said.

When he came back, Josh had lost the jacket and rolled up the sleeves on his dark blue button-down. He was smiling and rocking back and forth on the balls of his feet in the same way runners do before a race.

Carolyn noticed and asked, "Runner?"

He nodded. "Every morning, sunny or stormy," he replied.

"Well, I don't think either of us is dressed for it, but if you're ever up for a jog, I could always use the company," she said.

"I'll hold you to that," he replied, clicking the down button for the elevator.

"So, what can I do for you, Josh?" said Carolyn as the elevator door eased open again and they stepped in.

"Well, I've got something important I wanted to talk with you about, and I'm actually glad we can walk and talk at the same time. It helps me think, and it burns off the nervous energy."

"Nervous energy?" she asked.

"Yes," he replied. "Because I'm pretty sure I could lose my job by talking with you about this."

CHAPTER 30

MORAL COURAGE

"What do you mean, 'lose your job?'" Carolyn asked as the elevator door slid open and she and Josh made their way through the foyer and outside to the trail.

"Because I'm directly cutting around my boss to tell you this," said Josh. "But I don't know what else to do. Every time I bring it up, he shrugs it off like it's no big deal. But Mrs. Qualey, this is literally our biggest account, and we're messing up on it left and right. I'm afraid we're going to lose them . . . and soon."

"Maybe you should start at the beginning," said Carolyn. They'd reached the trail, and despite Josh's ominous tone, the late afternoon sunlight flickering through the trees was having a calming effect on her.

Josh nodded. "Of course," he said. "As I know you're aware, we have a handful of legacy clients that have worked with us for years, some for decades. Of those clients, Achebe & Associates is our biggest one, by far. They do a lot of class actions and SEC work that require extensive data consolidation, smart scanning, those kinds of things, and for the longest time, we were their sole document-processing provider. Over the past several months, however, they've had a lot of complaints, and for good reasons. Documents are being scanned and filed improperly, keyword-search functions are only catching half of what they should, and the overall quality of the work we're sending them is just downright abysmal. I know—I've seen it. I speak with them almost every other week about some issue or other, and all I can do is apologize, request a credit for them, and report it to my boss, but he's done nothing about it."

ON PRINCIPLE

IN DANGER

AS LONG AS IT TAKES

MORAL COURAGE IS STANDING FOR A PRINCIPLE IN SPITE OF KNOWN DANGER FOR AS LONG AS IT TAKES.

Josh shook his head and took a deep breath. "Today, I think, was the last straw. The owner's son, Akai Achebe, called me himself and said that our work product was no longer meeting their needs, and with no feedback—not even a call from a manager, let alone a department head or the CEO—they've decided to take their business elsewhere."

Josh stopped walking for a moment and locked eyes with Carolyn. "Mrs. Qualey, this is serious. If they leave . . . I don't know our organization's exact financial situation, but I'm pretty sure this is the shot that'll sink the ship."

Carolyn nodded thoughtfully. Inside, she was furious that no one let her know about the situation with the Achebes, and she was particularly upset with Crespo, the head of customer relations, for not providing her with information like this concerning any of their clients, legacy or otherwise. But she set that aside for a moment to acknowledge the fierce look of concern on Josh's face.

"I see," she said. "Thank you, Josh. It took an incredible amount of courage for you to come to me about this, and I can't thank you enough for letting me know that this is going on. I can't say I'm thrilled with the customer-relations department right now, but I'll cross that bridge immediately after I address this situation."

Josh nodded. "If it's okay to ask, what are you going to do?"

"I'm going to talk to the Achebes," said Carolyn. "And then I'm going to talk with Mr. Crespo. But first, I need to find out exactly what went wrong and then put everything we have into fixing it."

Josh seemed to brace himself before asking, "And are you going to tell Crespo how you found out about this?"

Carolyn nodded. "I am, and I'm going to make certain that he understands the severity of *not* addressing the Achebes' concerns and for not letting me know about them. And I'm going to point out how much moral courage it took for you to tell me about this. I'm impressed, Josh, I really am. You're right, some people may have fired you for cutting around your supervisor, but not me and not within the new Phossium we're working to create. You knew what was right, and you took initiative despite the possible consequences."

Josh smiled. "Thank you. I almost didn't come to you about it, but then you held that meeting about integrity and being intentional, and I just knew this was something I should do."

Carolyn smiled. "It was. And now I have to apologize to you, because I need to cut this walk short and get back to the office to make a very important phone call."

"Of course," said Josh. "If there's anything else I can do, please let me know."

"I will!" said Carolyn as she turned and began to jog back to the office. "And thank you again!" she said over her shoulder. She caught one last glimpse of Josh as she rounded the corner back to the office. His hands were in his pockets, and he seemed to be staring up into the tree line, lost in thought.

I'll have to follow up with him after this is over, she thought. *These are the kind of people we need working at Phossium— people who aren't afraid to stand for what's right on principle, regardless of the possible danger to themselves.*

CHAPTER 31

DANGER

Carolyn caught her breath on the elevator ride back to her office and almost sprinted to her desk. She didn't have many printed pieces of paper around her office—she tried to keep most of the info she needed on her computer—but her list of legacy client contact information was still in her top drawer from the introduction packages she'd sent a while back. And right there, at the top of the list, was the Achebe account.

She settled into her chair, took a deep breath, and dialed the number.

The line clacked a few times, and then a polite, warm voice on the other end said, "Akai Achebe, can I help you?"

"Mr. Achebe, I'm so glad I caught you. My apologies for the late hour," she said, noticing for the first time that it was just a little past seven o'clock. "This is Carolyn Qualey, the CEO of Phossium Enterprises, your document-processing company. I was hoping you might have a few minutes to speak with me."

Akai was silent for a moment, then said, "Mrs. Qualey, it is late and we're on a tight deadline for a big case. I would like to speak with you, however. Would you be available to meet tomorrow morning for about half an hour? Say around 6:30 a.m.?"

"Yes, of course," said Carolyn. She would have agreed to any time, but was surprised at the early hour.

SHE MAY NOT KNOW EXACTLY WHAT HAD HAPPENED, BUT **SHE WAS GOING TO FIND OUT EVERYTHING SHE COULD BEFORE SHE WALKED INTO THAT MEETING TOMORROW.**

"Great. We can get coffee at the Yeats Café on Third. See you then," he said and clicked off.

"See you then," said Carolyn into dead air, replacing the receiver. Well, she hadn't expected a warm reception by any means, but the fact that he was willing to speak with her in the first place was at least slightly encouraging.

She leaned back in her chair, cracked her knuckles, and began to pull up all the information she could find on the Achebe account. She may not know exactly what had happened, but she was going to find out everything she could before she walked into that meeting tomorrow.

CHAPTER 32

WHEN THINGS FALL APART

The Yeats Café was just around the corner from Phossium, so Carolyn got in early the next morning and walked over. She was still lost in thought when she stepped into the café, but before she had a chance to look around for Akai, she heard someone say, "Mrs. Qualey?"

She looked up. Standing in front of her was a young man in a light blue, tailored suit with a handsome leather satchel slung diagonally across his chest. He smiled when she looked up and extended his hand. "Akai Achebe," he said.

"Carolyn Qualey," she said, returning the handshake and smile. "Thank you so much for meeting with me. I apologize for the late call last night, but . . . well, let me buy you a coffee before we get into the details."

Carolyn was strongly aware of the half-hour time limit Akai had given her for the meeting, so with beverages in hand they sat down, and she jumped straight to the point.

"I'm not going to mess around with excuses, Mr. Achebe," she said. "Just know that I am deeply sorry for the quality of work your organization has received for some time and that I am personally giving you my word that this will not happen again. I'd like to speak with you about exactly what went wrong. Would you be willing to go over that with me?"

Akai glanced down at his watch and nodded. "Of course, though I'm not sure if I can get through all of it in half an hour."

"Any feedback is useful feedback, Mr. Achebe. Thank you," said Carolyn, pulling a notebook and pen from her purse and scribbling furiously as Akai dove into a quick assessment of the past few years of his company's relationship with Phossium.

At some points, Carolyn had to fight hard to keep her jaw from dropping. The quality of their work was downright appalling, and their customer service sounded just as bad. Of course, she'd been aware of many of the product-quality issues in general and had been working—she thought—with the department to correct several of them, but now she was kicking herself. She'd sent out the requests and received reports but hadn't had time for an in-person inspection; she'd simply expected her staff to tell her the truth.

Periodically, she would stop him to interject a question about a certain discrepancy or dive a little deeper into a conversation he'd had with a company representative, but overall she just let him talk as she took page after page of notes.

When Akai was done, she set down her pen and met his gaze.

"Thank you, Mr. Achebe," she said. "And from the bottom of my heart, I want to apologize to you and to your company for what you've had to go through. As of this moment, I can assure you that I'm taking personal responsibility for fixing every one of these issues—effective immediately—and that nothing like this will ever, ever happen again. With that in mind, I would humbly ask that you give our organization one last chance."

Akai's smile was almost apologetic as he said, "Thank you, Mrs. Qualey. It means a lot to me that you've approached me like this and that you've taken the time to listen to our concerns. But to be completely honest, it's too little, too late. I hope the feedback I've given you will help you as you work to improve your services, which it certainly sounds like you plan to do, but our firm can't wait for that day to come. We have a lot of people who depend on us and our ability to get results, and we can't afford to fail simply because we didn't have our paperwork straight."

He stood and reached out his hand. "I'm sorry. I know that's not what you wanted to hear, but we've made our decision. I wish you the best of luck."

ANY FEEDBACK IS USEFUL FEEDBACK, MR. ACHEBE. THANK YOU.

Carolyn shook his hand. "I understand. Thank you again for your time."

He nodded, and with a slight bow of the head, he turned and left.

Carolyn waited until he was out of sight and then sunk back into her chair and buried her face in her hands. That was it. As far as she was concerned, she'd just shut the doors on a three-decade-old business and kicked herself right out of a job.

CHAPTER 33

LET'S HOPE IT'S NOT TOO LATE

arolyn wasn't entirely sure what to do with herself when she got back to the office after her meeting with Akai Achebe. She flipped half-heartedly through the notes she'd taken, thinking about how useful these would have been a few months ago, or even a few weeks ago, when there was a chance she could have saved the organization. But as Akai had so clearly pointed out, today had been "too little, too late."

She glanced around her office. At least she'd achieved her dream of becoming a CEO, if only for a few months. It hadn't turned out at all like she'd imagined, but she'd done it. Her name had been on a door, and people had called her "boss" for a while.

She turned back to her computer and scrolled for a minute through the customer-relations database. As she did, a glimmer of hope slowly came to her. *Maybe I'm being too pessimistic about this*, she thought. *I couldn't save this account, but what if we can turn others around? What if it's not too late for them?*

It would take a week, if not two, for the news of the loss of the Achebe account to make it to Algus, making this the first and

only time Carolyn was glad for the organization's poor communication structure. In the meantime, if she could speak with other legacy customers and really turn them around, bring them back on board, and ensure them that they would have nothing but top-quality service from here on out, then maybe—just maybe—she could hold off the hand of fate and pull Phossium out of its tailspin.

The thought quickly sent her into action. Without a second to lose, she began firing off emails, sending an emergency meeting request to Batya, Raj, and Walsh, and pulling up every bit of information she could on customer complaints over the last few years, focusing on the largest accounts and working her way down, adding to the list everything she'd learned from Akai Achebe that morning.

She was deep into her assessment when she heard a knock at the door.

"Come in," she said, expecting to see Raj or Batya in early, but was surprised to see Josh standing in the doorway.

"Good time?" he asked.

She gave him a rueful grin. "Good as ever," she said.

He walked in and made his way over to one of the guest chairs where Carolyn noticed, for the first time, a stack of files and an old corduroy jacket flung over one of the arms.

"I just needed to grab my things from yesterday before I headed in," he said, and then asked, "How did it go yesterday?"

Carolyn sighed. "Not great, actually. The Achebes are done with us. Akai, Jelani's son, was kind enough to talk with me for a little this morning, but he was pretty clear that we're never getting their business back."

"Oh, man," said Josh, leaning back in surprise against the arm of the guest chair. "I'm so sorry. I should have come to you sooner, or done something sooner. They'd just been with us for so long that I thought there could still be a chance . . ." his voice trailed off.

Carolyn shook her head. "You did the right thing, Josh. We did what we could, and now we're going to have to find a way to work past this. The Achebes may have been our biggest account, but they weren't our only account. We still have a good list of people that we can start getting in contact with today and repairing relationships. Honestly, this is more my fault than anyone else's. I was so focused on fixing the problems we're having internally that I neglected our number-one priority: the customer."

She looked up then and gave an all-inclusive wave of her arm. "All of this, all of Phossium, exists for one purpose: to meet our customers' unmet needs, and so far, I've been failing miserably at this. It took you and one heck of a loss for me to realize this, but by God, I'm going to do everything in my power to fix this going forward."

A sudden knock at the door startled both of them.

"Come in," said Carolyn.

"We came as soon as we could," said Batya as she walked in, followed closely by Raj and Walsh and then stopped abruptly when she saw Josh standing in the room.

"Oh! I'm sorry, did we interrupt a meeting?" she asked.

"Not at all," said Carolyn. She started to introduce Josh, but Batya was already greeting him like an old friend, and Walsh had given him the "nod of acknowledgement."

After shaking hands all around, Josh said, "Great to see everyone, but I was actually on my way out. I have a couple of things I need to do today, but I'll be back in touch to see if there's anything else I can do. Mrs. Qualey, good luck," he added, then picked up his things and left.

"What did he mean by 'good luck?'" Walsh asked as the three of them took their seats.

"Well," said Carolyn, "I'll do my best to give you the condensed version."

She quickly ran through what had happened with Josh and the Achebes, and the potential impact.

"But I have a plan," she said, "and it starts with you, Batya. Did you bring your laptop?"

IT TOOK YOU AND ONE HECK OF A LOSS
FOR ME TO REALIZE THIS, BUT

BY GOD, I'M GOING TO DO EVERYTHING IN MY POWER TO FIX THIS GOING FORWARD.

Batya nodded and quickly scooped it out of the canvas satchel that hung from her shoulder.

"Great. I'm sending you a link now," said Carolyn. Then she turned to Walsh and Raj.

"I'm also going to need your help, but from a departmental perspective. I'm sending you a list right now of general customer complaints from the past year, starting with the ones from our largest and longest-running clients. I need the two of you to get together and start coming up with how we can address these issues in both document processing and customer relations. I've already written up several suggestions, but I need you to come up with some solid ideas and how we can start implementing them immediately. And please," she added, "the more interdepartmental solutions, the better. I'm sick and tired of these silos, and that mentality stops today."

Raj and Walsh stood up immediately.

"You got it," said Raj, and Walsh nodded in agreement. Together they walked out, Raj already talking through ideas with Walsh.

Carolyn looked back at Batya, who was busily reading through the link Carolyn had sent her.

"This is all of our customer-contact information," she said, looking up at Carolyn.

"Yup," said Carolyn. "We have some contacting to do."

CHAPTER 34

THIRD-ORDER QUESTIONS

"It's my fault," Carolyn reiterated to Batya as they scanned through the list together. "The customer should have been my priority from day one, but I failed to see that as clearly as I could have. But that changes today. Today, we start learning as much as we possibly can from our customers, doing our best to deeply understand their wants and needs, and then working with Raj, Walsh, and the rest of the Phossium team to make our work product excellent again."

Batya nodded as Carolyn spoke, only asking at one point if this new objective would replace her current focus on improving the culture.

Carolyn shook her head. "This isn't replacing our culture at all. In fact, it's part of it, which is something I should have been clearer about from the start. Focusing on our customer is what gives our culture a clear purpose," Carolyn explained. "Instead of existing for ourselves and having integrity simply so we can rely on each other to keep our word, we have to understand that Phossium exists primarily to meet the unmet needs of our customers. We go beyond ourselves to actively generate integrity, because we know that it has a direct impact on the customers' experience, and the derivative of that value-creation is beneficial to every single team member: The better the customer experience, the more we profit, which means more opportunities for career advancement, as well as better fringe benefits, incentives, bonuses—all that great stuff. It's an upward cycle that gains power with each rotation, as long as we're actively gener-ating it."

"Of course," said Batya. "Kind of like how a flywheel gains more stored energy the more torque you apply to it."

Carolyn arched a surprised eyebrow at Batya, who laughed. "I kind of have a thing for simple mechanics," she said.

"I'm not surprised," said Carolyn. "Yes, we gain across the board as long as our systems are functioning at their peak performance.

But first, we have to find out how and where we're failing. Hence, our project today."

With that, she picked up the phone, and as she dialed the first number on the list, she said to Batya, "I'm going to put this call on speaker so you can hear it, but don't say anything. I want this customer, Mr. Alvarez, to think that our conversation is completely between him and me. Just take notes and we can talk after the call, okay?"

Batya nodded, making the hand gesture for "my lips are zipped."

It took Carolyn a few minutes to get through to Alvarez, and when she did, she began by introducing herself and giving her reason for calling, which surprised Batya a little. It wasn't "to make things right" or "fix what's wrong," but rather "to get your feedback."

Alvarez grudgingly agreed to speak with her, and Carolyn thanked him for his time before diving right in.

"How are things going?" she asked, and his sharp reply made Batya wince. But Carolyn simply nodded, took a few notes, and then said, "I see. Thank you. And are you getting what you need?"

Again, the reply was bitter and short, but Carolyn took it in stride.

"I understand," she said when he finished, and then asked, "Is there anything we can do differently?"

Alvarez began listing off several of the issues he'd stated earlier, pointing out several things that could be improved, eliminated, or replaced.

All the while, Carolyn simply nodded or gave a word or two of affirmation, not offering any solutions but thanking him for his feedback. It was painful for Batya just to listen to, but Carolyn never flinched. She still wasn't done.

As he wrapped up his list of complaints, she thanked him once again and asked, "If you could, Mr. Alvarez, would you tell me what you're trying to do with your business, and what's making that hard for you?"

Alvarez hesitated a moment, perhaps not expecting that type of question, then shared with Carolyn the focus of his company and some of the broader challenges they were facing. To Batya, none of his answers seemed to pertain to their company, but Carolyn looked pleased as she jotted down note after note. Her next questions were also a little peculiar and almost seemed designed to provoke him.

Batya winced again as Carolyn said: "Tell me about anything we're providing you—and the way we're providing it—that is less than perfect," following that up with, "What would you want me to know about your and our companies' relationship?"

To Batya, it sounded like Carolyn was verbally walking up to a stake in a pile of kindling, tying herself to it, and asking her client to light the match—but at the same time, amidst the harsh criticism and personal attacks, Batya began to discern a deeper level of feedback. Still, it was painful to listen to, and as Alvarez wound down his answer to Carolyn's last question, Batya had to stop herself from audibly sighing in relief.

But Carolyn *still* wasn't done.

KEEP THE MAIN THING THE MAIN THING AND CUSTOMERS ARE THE MAIN THING.

"Thank you, Mr. Alvarez. I only have a few more questions, and again, I truly appreciate your time and honest feedback. Could you tell me, what would motivate you to refer us to one of your most trusted peers?"

The shocked silence should have been enough of an answer, but Carolyn waited patiently until Alvarez was able to muster the words, "Are you serious?" and then went from there. Her last two questions were just as open-ended and evocative:

"What would cause you to hesitate in any way to refer us to one of your most valued and trusted peers?" followed by, "What would the ideal partner—the absolutely ideal Phossium—look like to you?"

It was as difficult to listen to as it was to watch a train crash, but again, woven into the bitter words was a deeper and more authentic level of sharing than Batya could have hoped to draw out of one customer in a year. It was amazing, but at the same time, it seemed like an entirely lost opportunity. Carolyn was taking the feedback, studiously writing it down, but she wasn't offering even the slightest solution. And wasn't that what this was all about? Smoothing things over with the customer and bringing them back on track?

Finally, Carolyn thanked Mr. Alvarez one last time, assuring him that his feedback would be honored and that she would get back with him shortly. His goodbye was short, but Batya was a little surprised to also hear him thank Carolyn for the call.

Carolyn clicked off the speaker and looked at Batya expectantly, who could only shake her head in confused awe.

"That was incredibly difficult to listen to," she finally said to Carolyn. "I mean, sure, we got some really good feedback, but why didn't you take the opportunity to tell him what we could do about it? Why did you just thank him and leave it at that?"

"Have you ever heard the saying, 'Don't mix feedback with problem-solving?'" Carolyn asked.

Batya shook her head.

"That was my goal today," Carolyn explained. "Not to offer solutions, but to hear everything that Mr. Alvarez had to say about Phossium and his company's unmet needs. Now we need to be thoughtful in our response and honor his feedback so that when we go back to him—which we'll do very quickly—our responses will be well thought out, our staff will be completely prepared to commit to what we're going to promise our customers, and we'll be able to address all of his concerns with absolute integrity."

"I see," said Batya, feeling suddenly like it was her first day on the job and Carolyn was walking her through the essentials of customer relations in a way she'd never considered before. It wasn't that she'd never thought to try to find ways to learn as much as she could from her customers, but there was a power in what Carolyn had done, an intimacy that she'd created in finding ways to know her customer on such a deep level in such a short period of time.

With that thought, it dawned on Batya that this must be what it truly meant to lead. This was how Carolyn had been able to climb the corporate ladder over the years and why Algus had approached her to take over as Phossium's CEO. She'd learned the art of mastering customer feedback, and in doing so, she was able to speak with the voice of absolute authority in any business—the voice of the customer, which was stronger than the voice of the staff, the competitors, and the business leadership, combined.

It was a gift, Batya realized, that Carolyn shared with her today. The phone calls they were going to make were not going to be pleasant, but what she would derive from them, and the voice she would gain in speaking with those customers, would be her first real steps toward something beyond just being an employee—this was how one became a true leader.

"So, what do you think? Are you up for this?" Carolyn asked.

A slow smile lit across Batya's face as she said, "Yes, I—thank you. This isn't going to be the easiest thing I've ever done in my life, but thank you for showing me how to do it. Thank you for showing me how to really learn from our customers. I mean, there's no better way for a company to grow than to really understand our customers' actual wants and needs. There isn't anything much more powerful than that!"

Carolyn smiled. "Of course, Batya, and I'm glad you understand that. But before we jump on the phones again, let me explain a little more about this process. What I did with Mr. Alvarez just now was to ask him what are called 'third-order questions.' It's something I used to do at my former company, and it's hands-down the best way to discover the truth behind the customer's unhappiness with your company. You see, if I'd stopped at the first three questions, I'd only have scratched the surface. Mr. Alvarez answered them, but his replies were quick, off the cuff. By following up with the second set of questions, however, we were able to dig deeper."

Second-order questions, Carolyn said, were the "uncomfortable" questions; the ones that began with asking for outside-of-the-box information, such as "What are you trying to do with your business, and what's making that hard for you?"

"And then we move on to the third-order kind," Carolyn continued. "We thank them for their feedback and then say, 'Now I'd like to go deeper. What do you really wish you had in a service partner? This is not a criticism of us. Just because you can imagine something better doesn't mean we did anything wrong. Just describe your dream partner.' That is a third-order question, and that is the essence of what we're trying to get to today and over the coming days."

"Coming days?" Batya said apprehensively.

"Yes," said Carolyn. "We aren't going to get ahold of everyone today, and those that we do talk with will hopefully be on the phone with us for a while. But this is vital, Batya. If we don't understand our clients deeply, if we don't form intimate and authentic relationships with them, then we're lost. Last I looked, the customers were the ones paying us, not anyone else. These conversations—finding out their true needs and fulfilling them— are a matter of survival."

"But what if we can't get them all the way to third-order questions?" Batya asked. "What if they don't know how to answer the 'dream partner' question?"

"Good questions," said Carolyn. "Sometimes it's easier for people to talk about what's bothering them by using another person as an example. In psychology, it's called projection—where one is more comfortable projecting his or her own thoughts and feelings onto another person. For instance, if they can't get past their surface complaints, we can ask, 'I understand that you have these issues with our company, and I assure you we're going to address all of them, but we'd also like to make sure nothing like this ever happens again. To do that, I'd like to understand what you would tell me if I asked you about referring a very close friend of yours, or a loved one, to our company. What kinds of things would they need us to fix to provide them with the best experience possible?'"

Carolyn continued: "People often don't know how to criticize companies, but if you take their credibility off the line and allow them to project it onto someone else, it often becomes much easier for them to say what a partnering company should start— or stop—doing to motivate them to make that referral."

They spoke together for a few more minutes as Batya worked out the process. Then they both settled down with their lists, ready for the long haul and, deep down, excited to finally know what they needed to fix at Phossium and to make it right again.

CHAPTER 35

DISSOLVING THE DELUSION

n the end, it was almost a full week before Carolyn and Batya managed to connect with everyone on their contact lists.

There were various holdups, of course, from simply not being able to get ahold of someone to dealing with outright anger. There were times when both Carolyn and Batya were certain they were going to lose a customer by the end of a call, but they held in there, reassuring the customer that their feedback was being heard and acted on. Several times they went to Raj immediately afterward and asked him to assign a special task force to the customer—one of the solutions he and Walsh had worked out on day one—making sure their end product was both expedited and as close to flawless as humanly possible.

A follow-up call to Walsh, too, put him on alert about the same client, activating a customer-relations tactic that Walsh had devised. Carolyn actually suspected it was something he'd proposed a long time ago, but Crespo had either shot it down or completely ignored it.

The tactic was simple and astonishingly effective: Along with a handwritten note of apology (signed by Carolyn), document processing custom created an expedited timeline guaranteeing a quick project-completion date, as well as a printed update of their billing with new discounts or waived fees indicated. Finally, each client received a quality vacuum-insulated tumbler and a coffee shop gift card with the inscription "To help make up for any sleep you may have lost because of us."

Some days, especially early on, the progress was painfully slow, but as Carolyn and Batya grew to understand the customers more and began to anticipate their responses, their ability to actively listen and respond grew accordingly—and their running notes on how to improve the system became more and more refined.

Batya and Carolyn continued to meet regularly at the end of each day, reviewing what they'd learned and updating the online database they'd created for collecting customer feedback. The database was shared with Walsh and Raj as well, and occasionally, after a particularly heavy input day, one or both of them would drop by Carolyn's office with some fresh pastries or coffee from down the street and do a quick check-in.

It was on one of those evenings, toward the end of that brutal week, that Walsh made a unique observation about the customers' comments.

"You know, it's interesting reading what our customers have to say about what we're doing, but it's even more interesting to read about what they *think* we should be doing," Walsh said between bites of blueberry scone.

"How do you mean?" asked Carolyn.

"Well," said Walsh, "they're pretty concrete on where we've gone wrong with their services in the past, but when they talk about what they expect, it looks like they're saying it in a couple different ways."

He put down his pastry, quickly wiped his hands off on a napkin, and pulled the latest database printout toward him, leaving it on the small side table they were sharing so they could all see what he meant.

"See here?" he said. "This guy says the quality of the work is so bad that it makes his company look ridiculous, and he expects us to fix it quickly and with unequivocal perfection."

He thumbed through a couple pages and then pointed at another one.

"This person here says the quality of our work proves that we have no idea what we're doing and that we better bring in some people who do, and fast, or they're out."

Then, on the same page, he pointed to another line.

"And here, this guy states that the number of correctly completed work orders has dropped 15 percent since he started with us five years ago, and he expects that number not only to go back up to what it was before, but to achieve at least 95 percent clarity and accuracy."

Walsh looked up at the other three, who just stared at him blankly. He huffed a little in exasperation.

"Don't you see? The first two are criticizing our services based on emotions, while the last guy tells us what happened in *fact*, and what he expects in *fact*."

Carolyn spun the pages toward her and looked again at what Walsh had read to them. He was right. The vast majority of the comments were based on emotions; they were stories and beliefs about Phossium's work and the clients' expectations, whereas a small handful of clients stated direct facts.

When it came to statements of fact, Carolyn could see exactly what needed to be done to make the client happy, but the emotional statements—the stories and beliefs—just fostered more emotion and didn't give them any real direction on what to do about the situation.

The difference in how the clients addressed *them* probably couldn't be helped, she thought, but in seeing the various ways in which the clients conveyed their needs flicked on a light bulb in Carolyn's mind.

If everyone at Phossium learned to master conversation through the conveyance of *fact*, they could be vastly clearer about what they were doing and what they expected to be done. Shoot, they would be far clearer about *everything*. It would engender cohesion between people and departments, foster integrity, and finally, help lead to the kind of alignment—the interconnectedness and interdependency—that they so desperately needed to achieve.

TO COMMUNICATE WITH THE MOST CLARITY, WE NEED TO **FOCUS ON SHARING INFORMATION BASED ON FACTS, NOT STORIES OR BELIEFS.**

She turned to the other three with the brightness of revelation written across her face.

"Of course," she said excitedly. "That's it, that's exactly what we need to do!"

Now it was Walsh's turn to look confused.

"Do what?" he asked. "I just thought it was interesting . . . ."

Carolyn waved her hand dismissingly. "You're right, it is, and that's what got me thinking . . . ."

She jumped up and grabbed a blank sheet of paper from her printer, stopped at her desk, and scribbled on it with a marker. Then she came back and put the paper on the table. In big, bold letters she'd written:

Stories

Beliefs

Facts

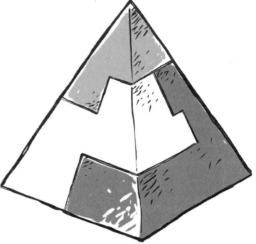

"You see," she explained, "the first statement Walsh read was a story. The customer was just giving his opinion and ascribed his own meaning to the impact of a poor work product." She turned to the complaints sheet and highlighted the first statement, circling the phrases "look ridiculous" and "unequivocal perfection."

"The second statement was more of a belief," she continued. "Their experience tells them that it's possible to do better and that this requires people who know what they're doing to do it. This is a kind of truth based on experience, but not on evidence, not on fact—so it's still a little harder to tell what they specifically need."

She highlighted that statement and then the last one Walsh had read.

"This statement," she said, "provides us with solid fact. It tells us where we are and exactly what they expect to make it better. In conveying what they need with facts, we know exactly how to take action and get things done."

She looked at all of them expectantly. Raj was the first to speak up.

"So, what you're saying," he said, his brow furrowed in concentration, "is that, to communicate with the most clarity, we need to focus on sharing information based on facts, not stories or beliefs."

"Yeah," said Batya, her face brightening as she grasped the idea, "and we need to be able to tell the difference when we hear others speaking, whether it's internally or coming from clients. If we can help others learn how to share facts that can be acted on, then that brings us onto the same page—we know what's expected, and they know what they're expecting. It's alignment," she said, smiling. "It's alignment internally between each other and externally with our customers."

Walsh, stony expression firmly set, glanced among the three of them.

"I would have thought that everyone understood the importance of speaking in facts," he said. "How else does anything ever get done?"

"I would never expect anything different from you, Walsh," Carolyn said with a grin. "But you're one in a million. So many people speak with emotion these days that it's often hard for most of us to tell the difference. If we focus on the difference, however, we *will* be able to get much more done."

With that, she scooped up the papers on the table, tucked them into a manila folder that she then tossed onto her desk, and then turned to the other three with a "shooing" gesture.

"Now, out. Go home. It's late, and I think we've exhausted our revelations for the night. We've still got a lot of work ahead of us, but we're making progress every day, thanks to all of you," she said.

Raj, Batya, and Walsh nodded in agreement, picked up their bags and leftover pastries and coffees, and wished her good night.

Carolyn walked them to the door, waved good night, and then turned to grab her own work satchel and car keys. As painful and exhausting as the last couple of weeks had been, they had also been rewarding in their own way. She felt like she was gaining a far deeper understanding of her customers than she ever had before, and in knowing exactly what actions were needed to turn dissatisfaction into appreciation, and how to convey that in a highly accurate way to a team that was getting closer and closer to working seamlessly together, she felt a welling up of strength that stretched far beyond herself.

Phossium was becoming less and less a set of disjointed parts and more and more one interconnected and positively aligned force.

CHAPTER 36

POSSIBILITIES

The next day, and for the first time since she'd started at Phossium, Carolyn went home shortly after five o'clock. and told Raj, Walsh, and Batya to do the same. They'd be able to meet on customer feedback more the following day. Tonight, she had something more important to do.

Most nights, by the time Carolyn made it home, she barely had the energy to heat up a frozen dinner before stumbling wearily into bed, but tonight she pulled a couple of nice steaks from the fridge and rubbed them down with a sprinkle of salt and pepper, letting them warm up to room temperature as she prepared a somewhat labor-intensive asparagus risotto.

She was just adding the last splash of chicken stock to the risotto when she heard the front door open, followed by the bump and thud of luggage being dragged in and dropped by the stairs. She quickly cut the heat down on the stove and, just as she was turning around, felt a strong pair of arms wrap around her waist and a bristly chin rub against her neck.

She spun around and wrapped her arms around her husband, kissing him and then cuddling her face into the crook of his neck, which was as far as her five-foot-eight height reached on his six-foot-two frame.

"Welcome home, babe," she said, holding him tightly.

He squeezed her in his arms and kissed the top of her head.

"It's great to be home," he replied.

She stayed there for just a moment, enjoying the peace of his arms, then pulled back a little and wrinkled her nose, looking at him with a playful smile.

"Guess you didn't get a chance to bathe on that nineteen-hour trip home, huh?" she said.

He laughed and pulled her back toward him, pretending to rub his sweaty shirt on her nose. "Not at all. I think it makes me manlier," he said, smiling.

"Ah!" she laughed, pushing him away. "Upstairs; shower; now. Dinner will be ready in fifteen, so make it quick."

He kissed the top of her head again and nodded. "Just for you, I'll rinse off," he said, turning to go upstairs.

"Use soap!" She shouted after him as he vanished up the stairs with his suitcase.

David dug into his favorite dinner as though he hadn't eaten a decent meal in months—which Carolyn suspected was likely the case. And if she was honest with herself, she couldn't remember the last time she'd had a home-cooked meal, either.

For a while, the only sounds in the room were the melodic arrangements of the Bill Evans Trio interspersed with the clink of cutlery on porcelain. It wasn't until they were both about halfway through their meals that they began talking, and even then, they kept it general, David talking about the beautiful countrysides he was able to visit and the antics of his coworkers, and Carolyn sharing the lighter side of her day-to-day—morning jogs, afternoon walks, generalities about her office work, and getting to know Batya and Raj, as well as how surprising a character Hugh Walsh had turned out to be. She updated him on their children, as well: Sadie had called a few more times from school just to let her know how classes were going and to assure her mom that she was still alive, and she told him about a rare call from Gus, who sounded well, though she could never quite keep the worry completely out of her voice, especially around David.

David was glad to hear all of it, especially about Sadie and Augustus, and told her he'd been in touch with Sadie a little here and there as well, though the time difference made it harder for them to catch up.

It wasn't until they'd finished the meal, cleared the dishes, and curled up on the couch with some wine that they delved into the harder stuff. Carolyn let David go first; she wasn't in any hurry to share the details of the roller coaster she'd been on for the last four months.

His latest project was a rather large office building in Dubai that he'd designed specifically for his client. It was an elegant master-piece of subtle, sensual curves set against stark, powerful lines that spoke to an almost regal mindset—a sense of being greater and more important than any of the surrounding buildings, even though it was smaller than some by several stories.

It had taken David almost two years to design it, another year to refine it and get the final approval from the owner and his firm, and a year and a half more to get all of the permitting in order. It was only in the past six months that actual construction had begun, and David had been right there, from the day they broke ground to the installation of the substructure's massive concrete piers and the initial formation of the steel skeleton.

He told her about the challenges they'd run into, from bad batches of concrete to sloping bedrock and complications with the anticipated placement of mechanical versus electrical systems. Fortunately, he explained, his site superintendent pointed this out to him early on, allowing him to redesign the systems before they got to the actual installation.

Carolyn listened with fascination. Considering everything she'd learned in the recent months about communication and alignment, integrity and interconnectedness, she was surprised to discover that her husband was already embracing all of these ideals, even though he didn't call them by those names. He spoke about being "on the same page" as his head project manager, head engineer, and site superintendent, for instance, but he didn't talk about them being "in alignment." It was almost like he took it for granted that they spoke the same language and were in pursuit of the same goal: a building both beautiful and solidly built that their customer would love.

She was so deep in these thoughts that she only half heard what he was saying until she heard him say, ". . .which is why we always call them 'possibilities.'"

She looked up and eyed him quizzically.

"What did you say?" she asked.

He laughed. "Guess my story wasn't as riveting as I thought it was."

She shook her head and gave him an apologetic smile. "I'm sorry, Hon, I'm listening. I just missed that last part. You said you called them 'possibilities.' What was 'them?'"

David shifted in his seat and set his remaining half glass of wine down on the ash-and-iron coffee table so he could talk the way he always did when he was excited: with his hands.

"Problems," he explained, his hands making an all-encompassing gesture. "We call problems 'possibilities,' because it allows us to think of them as that; as opportunities. Like the concrete I was telling you about earlier. We didn't realize we had a bad batch until one of our workers pointed out that someone had added regrind to the mix, which was severely weakening it. We immediately stopped pouring and had to remove all the concrete we'd already poured, which was a huge delay. However, in the process of finding a reliable replacement, we learned about this new carbon-fiber-reinforced concrete that is not only stronger than the concrete we were using, but is more durable, more moldable, and even recyclable."

"What's more," he added, "this concrete is allowing us to re-envision some of the more aesthetic outer aspects of the building, making it possible to shape the more complex curves with less materials while keeping it just as durable, if not more so."

Looking like a maestro conducting his orchestra, David's hands whisked through the air as he described the pouring of the concrete, its removal, and the anticipated lines and curves of his building.

Carolyn was impressed, though she still questioned him out of habit.

"How do you know this stuff will work better, though? If it's that new, then couldn't there be some unexpected problems later on?"

David gave her a wry grin. "Always the skeptic. But you're right. It's never a good idea to completely accept new things at face value. We went and spoke with a nearby carbon-fiber-concrete manufacturing company while the old concrete was being removed, and we also had it tested by three different labs. Turns out it's as good as they said it was. But if we do run into a 'problem' later, I believe it will just open the door to another possibility."

"That sounds suspiciously like hopeless optimism," Carolyn said, to which David replied by tossing a throw pillow at her.

"There's optimism and then there's realism," he said. "We took our optimistic solution and realistically tested it six ways from Sunday. Turned out, that product was a solution we hadn't even thought to look for yet. But if we'd looked at it as a problem, we likely wouldn't have taken the opportunity to look outside of the box. We would have just brought in a new batch of concrete, checked it for regrind, and started pouring again. Problem solved.

"Instead, by looking for possibilities, we found a product that's going to have a huge impact on this project, as well as on any of the designs I do going forward."

While David was talking, Carolyn picked up her wine glass from where she'd set it on the side table and swirled it a little, looking thoughtfully down into its garnet depths as he spoke. She heard rather than saw David get up and grab the bottle, bringing it back to top off both of their glasses. She didn't mind, even though she usually limited herself to just one glass. Tonight was a celebration, after all.

After a few minutes she heard him say, "Penny for your thoughts."

"I'm sorry?" She looked up, startled.

"Either you think that wine needs some serious aerating, or there's something on your mind," he said.

She smiled softly and looked back down at her glass, finally taking a sip and setting it down again.

"I'm just thinking about what you said," she said. "About what's possible. It's not only a matter of semantics, like you said. It's decisive. When an action is being called for from the context of 'Something is wrong and we need to fix this,' what becomes available for you is constrained by the nature of the problem. So, when the problem is fixed, you end up with what you had and not much more.

"But when you face an unexpected event from the context of 'What is possible here?' then you can be fully free in your choice of actions. They're not constrained by the boundaries of the problem."

"Exactly," said David, "though you put that far more eloquently than I ever could."

"So, what's possible?" she said, looking at him openly. "That's the next question we need to be asking. What's possible for our customer? What's possible for the staff? What's possible, period? It's just a matter of reorienting our thought process, which we're already doing plenty. But, if we start

IF WE START USING 'POSSIBILITY' AS OUR CONTEXT, **THEN WHO KNOWS WHAT INNOVATIONS OR GROWTH WE COULD SEE AT PHOSSIUM?**

using 'possibility' as our context, then who knows what innovations or growth we could see at Phossium?"

She got up and started pacing the room, ticking thoughts off on her fingers. "Forget problems. Going forward, regardless of circumstance, we need to look at it as 'what's possible?'"

David, watching her from the couch, gave her a bemused grin. "I take it you're still dealing with quite a few 'possibilities' at the new job, huh?"

She stopped mid-pace and gave him a half-smile, then walked over and hopped onto the couch, leaning against him as he draped a shower-fresh arm across her shoulders

"You could say that," she said, and finally launched into everything that had happened since the last time they spoke.

It was nearing midnight by the time they'd completely caught up with each other, and it wasn't until Carolyn caught David nodding off, almost spilling what was left of the wine in his hand, that she declared it bedtime. Together they trudged up the stairs and fell asleep, deeply and peacefully, in each other's arms for the first time in a long time.

CHAPTER 37

FAULTY PARTS

What's possible. The thought stayed with Carolyn all morning as she got ready for work, wished David a good day, and drove to the office. She was still thinking about it as she walked upstairs, and as she reached the fourth floor, she realized she'd come to one very certain conclusion.

If Phossium was going to reach new levels of customer-service excellence, if they were going to look beyond the immediate and work together to achieve what was possible, then she had to make sure they were all in it together, and there were two pieces of the current system that she knew for a fact would not be on board. She'd hesitated for a long time to do it, primarily because of Dolores's assertion that all the department heads needed to remain in place, but after their last conversation, Dolores's opinion had lost all sway with Carolyn. She knew what she had to do: Marsalis Crespo, the head of customer relations, and Bob Quills, the head of document processing, had to go.

It wouldn't exactly come out of the blue for either of them. She'd spoken with both on multiple occasions about the isolationist attitude they'd taken regarding their departments and toward the company as a whole, and although she'd personally invited both of them to the internal talk she'd given on culture, neither had bothered to attend or had even responded. That, on top of what she'd heard from Akai Achebe and the other clients she and Batya spoke with, was the nail in the coffin. She couldn't have faulty parts in this system. She'd explain this all to them, of course, and give them the chance to align their departments with the new culture, but she suspected her proposal might not be received well.

She was right.

She arranged for meetings with both Quills and Crespo that day, setting up her first meeting with the head of document processing. Bob Quills had been with the company for about ten years and had basically been given free reign over his department. Oz, the former owner, had rarely checked in with him, except maybe to share the occasional snifter of brandy, and, consequently, Bob took the same isolationist attitude with her, despite her efforts to get him to open up and interact with her on the department's progress. What info she did get from him was piecemeal, and most of the status requests she sent seemed to vanish as though into a black hole.

She walked into her appointment with him that day, not with the curious respect she'd afforded him in the past, but with authority. She explained first about the feedback she'd received from Achebe & Associates and personally from Akai Achebe, as well as how many of their customers felt, citing the well-known statistic that, for every unhappy customer who complains, there are twenty-six others who don't. [2]

From there she shared with him, briefly but powerfully, the concept of integrity and the need for everyone in the company to be both intentional and persistent in generating it; that they would have to maintain it every day, but in doing so they would create an environment in which each of them could work at their peak performance levels—which meant the company worked at its peak performance level.

"This company," she concluded, "needs to be functioning as one interconnected, interdependent unit with the clear goal of ensuring that every action we take part in has an unobstructed line of sight in meeting our customers' unmet needs. If you can't see that, if you can't get on board with that and get your department functioning at levels along with the rest of us, then I have no choice but to let you go."

FROM THERE SHE SHARED WITH HIM, BRIEFLY BUT POWERFULLY, THE CONCEPT OF INTEGRITY AND **THE NEED FOR EVERYONE IN THE COMPANY TO BE BOTH INTENTIONAL AND PERSISTENT IN GENERATING IT.**

2   Colin Shaw, "15 Statistics That Should Change the Business World—But Haven't," *LinkedIn* (June 4, 2013): https://www.linkedin.com/pulse/20130604134550-284615-15-statistics-that-should-change-the-business-world-but-haven-t.

Bob chose to go, packing up his desk in front of her and promising to let his good friend, Dolores Pendergrast, know about her actions immediately.

Carolyn gave him a rueful smile. "You're welcome to do just that, Mr. Quills. Let her know I said 'hello.'"

One down, one to go: Her next difficult meeting was with the head of customer relations.

Through her own experience and, more recently, through her direct customer conversations, it hadn't taken Carolyn long to learn that Marsalis Crespo ran what could only be described as an isolated feudal system, leaving the heavy lifting to his subordinates and refusing either to create reports or to respond to information requests. His word was law, and if a customer wasn't happy with a reply, then that was that. If they complained, he rarely acknowledged it; and if they left, well, that just meant a little more peace and quiet for him.

Again, Carolyn had been largely unaware of this problem until she'd spoken with Akai, and only learned about the true breadth and depth of it after speaking with their remaining customers.

It was the same talk, same approach, same opportunity to turn it around that she'd given Quills, but at the end of it, Crespo simply eyed her up and down and said, "You sure think you're something, don't you? Wish I could be there on the day these hot little ideas of yours burn you to the ground."

Carolyn simply arched a questioning eyebrow at him.

"So, I take it you don't care to work with me on bringing transparency to this department? On bringing it in line and interconnected with the rest of Phossium?" she asked.

"You dig your own grave, Carolyn. I've been putting up with your little demands and pointless meetings for long enough. There are plenty of other companies that would have me, and pay me more, besides. I was comfortable here, but that sun started setting when you arrived," he said, pushing his wide girth back in his chair. "No, I don't care to work with you. I'll be out of here by the end of the day."

She nodded.

"I'd say I understand, but I don't. I wish you luck," she said as she got up to leave.

Crespo didn't say a word; just turned the back of his chair to her and began typing as if she weren't in the room.

She left Crespo's office with mixed feelings. She was glad that those difficult conversations were over with, but she regretted not being able to convince at least one of them that this new approach would benefit everyone in the company, including himself.

But people, in general, do not like to change. She knew this. She also knew that there were times when she was going to have to stand strongly by the changes she knew needed to be made without flinching, and she felt she'd done just that.

Just then, the words of a long-ago speech by Martin Luther King Jr., which she'd memorized decades ago, came rushing back to her, more fiercely poignant today than they'd ever been:

"It is possible to stand up against an unjust system with all of your might, with all of your body, with all of your soul, and yet not stoop to hatred and violence. Something about this approach disarms the opponent. It exposes his moral defenses, weakens his morale, and at the same time, works on his conscience."

Both Crespo and Quills had been shaken by her authoritative stance, and in working on their consciences, it occurred to both that they could not stand to work in the environment she was proposing. They could not live in a place where they were held accountable for both their own and their department's actions, where their systems were laid bare and they were forced to work within a team construct as opposed to commanding others within their self-made dictatorships.

By Carolyn's standing for integrity, two of the faulty parts that were impeding the peak performance of Phossium fell away, which left her with a cleaner system but also with two significant functions to fill.

Fortunately, she knew just whom she needed to talk to.

CHAPTER 38

THE RISE OF RAJ AND WALSH

arolyn could hear the soft murmur of chatter coming from the newly filled office space as she walked past her office and down the hall. One wall, which fronted the hallway, was made of floor-to-ceiling frosted glass, and beyond it she could see vague shadows moving in and between the unmoving hulks of office equipment, softly illuminated by what looked like several sources of light at varying heights.

She knocked on the door and heard a hearty "Come on in!" as she swung the door open.

There had to be at least twenty people in the room, half at their desks and the other half diligently plugging, poking, adjusting, and fiddling with six mammoth copy machines lined up against the back wall. Several more people were setting up what looked like a command center right in the middle of the machine row, with stacks of fresh paper, rows of recycling bins, binding materials, pens, sticky tabs, folders, dividers, and everything else needed to complete physical end products, while a few others were connecting laptops to each copy machine and apparently running compatibility tests.

The rest of the room was sitting in the community-desk formation that Carolyn now immediately associated with Raj—desks facing each other to create an open, collaborative workspace. Some team members had their headphones on and were working intently on projects, while a few others were conversing happily across the table. Raj, of course, was bantering right along with them, though Carolyn could see what looked like dozens of work orders open on his screen. Raj stood up as she walked in and waved her over.

"Mrs. Qualey, it's great to see you! What do you think of the room?" he said, sweeping his arms out to indicate their new space.

"Looks like you're moving right in," she said with a smile. "Where are the thermometers?" she asked, remembering how his team used to keep track of document-processing progress for each customer in their old office.

Raj grinned. "I'm glad you asked. Check it out," he said, and with that he bent down and typed a quick command into his laptop. "Sharon, would you get the lights?" he asked one of the team members.

"Way ahead of you," she said, stepping quickly to the other side of the room. She flicked the overhead light switch and instantly the room was filled with a soft, soothing light. Carolyn noticed for the first time that there were lamps everywhere—on desks, tables, cabinets, standing in corners, and even a few hanging from the ceiling. The soft light was a soothing reprieve from the harsh overhead fluorescents and automatically reminded her of her own desk lamp back in her office.

Then Raj clicked another button and suddenly the walls were filled with real-time images of thermometers, several with visibly rising mercury while others held at neutral, and some appeared to be dropping. The name of each account was written parallel to its image in an artistic font. After a second, Carolyn noticed that the few that were nearing full were glowing brighter than the others.

"How . . . ?" she started to ask, and Raj pointed to a small white box on the community table. It was a mini projector, one of three carefully positioned throughout the room.

"I've had these for a while, just never had the space to use them. The progress of each thermometer is a live feed from its account. As each task is completed, the thermometer rises, and if a customer needs something redone, the thermometer falls, indicating that we need to go back and fix it. Overall, it means less paper waste and arts-and-crafts effort on our part . . . and it makes for a pretty neat show," he said with a smile.

He clicked the images off, and Sharon flipped the bright fluorescents back on. They all winced a little in the sharp artificial glare.

WE COULD HAVE ALL THE INTEGRITY IN THE WORLD BUT, AS WE'VE ALL COME TO UNDERSTAND —OVER THE PAST WEEK, ESPECIALLY— **WE'RE NOTHING WITHOUT OUR CUSTOMERS.**

"Once we have all the equipment up and running, we'll keep the lamps on and the overheads off. It's just more comfortable to work in natural light," Raj explained.

Carolyn nodded. "I'm very impressed. That thermometer display is something else! How did you come up with it?"

Raj pointed to one of the team members working on systems checks. "Not me! Kevin Zhang over there is the graphics whiz. He's one of the new guys on the team. He took one look at the thermometers on the wall downstairs, and the next day he showed me this. The guy's a genius!"

Kevin looked up from his computer and waved, then ducked back into his work.

Raj gave a half-apologetic smile. "He's not super social, but he's great at what he does."

Carolyn shook her head. "No apologies needed. I think it's amazing, and it looks like he's comfortable here. Are the other team members integrating well?"

Raj nodded. "For sure. I mean, we haven't been in here long, but everyone seems to be getting along well. We all have our particular talents, and so far, no one's really clashing on anything."

"Good to hear," said Carolyn. "And speaking of changes, I was wondering if I could speak with you for a minute back in my office?"

"Of course," said Raj. "Let me wrap up a couple of things and I can be there in ten. Is that okay?"

Carolyn nodded. "Perfect. I'll see you then." Then, in a slightly louder voice she said, addressing the room, "And thank you all for your hard work here. The room looks great, and I look forward to some more 'full-thermometer' parties!"

There was a murmur of "Thanks!" from the room, accompanied by several smiles and waves as she left the room.

Back in her own office, Carolyn picked up the phone and dialed down to the second floor. After a few short rings, it picked up.

"Walsh," said the gruff voice on the other end.

"Hugh, it's Carolyn," she said. "Do you have a minute to swing upstairs to my office?"

"Sure," he said. "On my way." And clicked off.

A few minutes later, both Raj and Walsh came in at the same time. They'd apparently run into each other in the hallway, and Raj was laughing at something Walsh had said. That rare smile had once again lit across Walsh's face, giving him the look of a far younger—and kindlier—man.

Both men looked up at Carolyn and greeted her with a smile as she welcomed them in, gesturing for them to take a seat in the guest chairs as she walked around to lean comfortably against the front of her desk.

"I know neither of you really knows why I've asked you here on such short notice," she began, diving right into it, "but this company isn't at a stage of recovery and growth where we can act slowly."

She saw Raj's brow knit with mingled curiosity and concern while Walsh reverted to his habitual stony expression.

She paused. "In fact, that wasn't as clear to me as it should have been from the beginning. I came in here, guns a-blazing, determined to repair what seemed to be a broken and dejected environment. I wanted people to care about their jobs and trust the people they work with, and I thought that by fixing that, by engendering this trustworthy culture founded on the principle of integrity, we'd fix everything. But I was wrong."

Raj's expression remained unchanged. Walsh raised a questioning eyebrow but remained silent.

She went on. "We could have all the integrity in the world, but as we've all come to understand—over the past week, especially— we're nothing without our customers. However, we cannot give our customer our best if our *system* is not working at its best. If we're not in alignment, then our system is not running efficiently, which affects our end product, which directly affects our customers. So, to that end, I've had to make some adjustments to the mechanism and remove some faulty parts."

She explained the conversations she'd had with both Quills and Crespo that morning, and a look of clarity came rushing over Raj's face. Walsh, however, remained resolute in his impenetrable expression.

"That explains a lot," said Raj. "I heard Quills went storming out of here this morning, but I honestly didn't think a lot of it. He's not . . . well, he's not the calmest person in the world."

Carolyn nodded. "He seemed pretty fired up, and I'm sure I'm going to hear about it from on high sooner rather than later. But in the meantime, I'd like to ask the two of you if you would be willing to step into their old positions. Raj, would you take Quills's old job as head of document processing, and Walsh, would you replace Crespo as head of customer relations?"

She stopped then and left the question hanging in the air.

Raj nodded, his brow furrowed even deeper and his hands clasped tightly over his knees. Walsh looked down, a look of deep contemplation on his face. After a moment, Raj looked up and said, "I have to be honest with both of you: I've actually been considering leaving this company for some time."

Carolyn felt her heart hit her feet like a stone, but she kept her peace and let him continue.

"Long before you started here, Mrs. Qualey, I felt like anything I did was like throwing pebbles into a bottomless pit in the hopes of filling it up. Sure, we eventually got a good little group going, and I was able to get some independence under Crespo, but it was far from fulfilling."

He stood up and walked around behind his chair, leaning against it with an anxious air before continuing, "Even after you started, Mrs. Qualey, I felt like there wasn't much opportunity here, and while the new office space and new team members were nice, I still didn't feel right here. In fact," he looked her directly in the eyes, "I've been offered another position at another firm, and I was going to talk with you about that today."

Carolyn fought the sick feeling in the pit of her stomach and forced herself to appear calm.

"I see," she said, "and I understand. We're in a tenuous place right now, and I know you have a family to look out for. If there's anything . . ." she began, but Raj cut her off.

"I was going to talk with you about it today, Mrs. Qualey, because I wanted you to know about the offer. But after really taking the time to think about what you're trying to do here—what we're all trying to do here—and what's truly possible with this organization, I want you to know that I've decided to stay. And I can't tell you how honored I am that you're offering me this position, even without knowing that I was considering another job."

He held her gaze for a moment, letting her know that he understood the full weight of his decision. Carolyn's heart soared as she reached out and shook Raj's hand heartily.

"My heavens, Raj, you about gave me a heart attack," she said, relief washing over her.

Raj laughed. "I didn't mean to worry you. I just wanted you to know. I'd much rather stay here and take on this challenge. I mean, where could I find a better team to work with?" he said, smiling.

Carolyn shook her head with a smile and patted him on the shoulder. "You're something else, Raj. Thank you. I've lost about five years off my life, but thank you," she smiled, then turned to Walsh. "You're not planning to take another five years from me, too, are you? I don't think I have that many left."

Hugh stared hard at her for a moment, then suddenly emitted a short, explosive snort and broke into a jovial grin. *God help me*, she thought, *is that a laugh?*

"I'm with Raj here. I'm incredibly honored. And yes, I gladly accept the position . . . on the grounds, though, that we mutually agree on how we're going to continue to straighten out these departments. No harebrained ideas coming out of left field that we have to implement without question, right?" he said.

Carolyn couldn't help but laugh, clear and unbridled. She shook Walsh's hand and smiled at both of them.

"Hugh, you are a man of many surprises," she said. "Yes, I absolutely promise you that any major decisions regarding your department—or any department in this company—will be discussed in full. I'll need everyone's input, as well as a wealth of knowledge regarding this company's history, to make the best decisions possible. Anything that one person in this company does either directly or indirectly impacts everyone else, on every level. We have to keep that in mind at all times. We're an inter-connected, interdependent system, and our function from this day going forward is to be driven by our customer."

CHAPTER 39

JOSH RETURNS

I t didn't feel like it had been just over a week since the news dropped about the Achebes. So much had changed in such a short period of time that Carolyn felt like she was running an entirely different company. And in a way, she was.

For one, she was no longer alone when she walked into the office early. On any given day there were at least a few other cars in the parking lot: team members who came in early to get a jump on their work because they wanted to, not because someone had asked. And at the end of the day, she was waving good night to more and more night owls who were sticking around for the same reasons. It wasn't that she encouraged working beyond regular office hours, but those who did knew that they had the flexibility to come and go as they needed to; they weren't held to a strict punch-in, punch-out policy. They were there because they wanted to be there, and that alone told Carolyn that Phossium was finally headed in the right direction.

Sitting down at her computer for the day, Carolyn quickly scanned her emails to see if the news of the Achebe account had reached Algus. At this point, she was wavering between telling them now or waiting until the quarterly meeting the next day to inform them about it. In fact, it would be better if she could do it tomorrow, as it would give her a chance to share some of the positive results that she, Batya, Walsh, and Raj were already starting to show with their customers. Not a lot, of course—it was still early in the process—but they were already receiving the first glimmers of positive feedback from the new systems they were implementing, and she hoped that very soon those glimmers would turn into full-on satisfied customers and a much-needed uptick in work orders.

She was just getting ready to review the latest reports from the team when she heard a knock on her door and looked up to see Josh walking through the doorway before she could even say "Come in." His face was flushed as he rushed up to her desk and dropped a thin, stapled document in front of her.

"You won't believe it," he said, sounding as though he'd sprinted up all four flights of stairs on his way to her office.

"I won't believe what, Josh? Are you okay?" she asked.

He shook his head. "I'm fine, I'm fine. This," he tapped his index finger on the papers he'd given her. "You're not going to believe this. The Achebes are back, and they've placed one heck of an order!"

CHAPTER 40

DOING WHAT YOU KNOW TO BE RIGHT

arolyn was having a hard time processing what Josh was saying. They'd lost the Achebe account. Akai had been incredibly clear about that. But as she looked down at the document in front of her, she saw a work order for . . . .

"*How* much?" she said, actually rubbing her eyes and rereading the order.

Josh was grinning from ear to ear.

"I . . . how did you . . . ?" She stopped, took a deep breath, and took a second to compose herself. Then she looked at Josh and, in a voice filled with both perplexity and amazement, said, "Josh, this is too amazing to be true! What happened? How did this happen? Sit down, tell me everything."

Josh, still smiling, sat down in the guest chair and took a deep breath.

"Well, it all started that day you told me we lost the Achebe account. I felt responsible for it. I knew I'd done all I could as far as my role in customer relations went, but I felt that I could do more. So, I made a phone call," he explained.

That phone call had been to Akai, whom Josh had gotten to know over the past several months due to their customer-relations interactions. Despite the poor results, Josh knew Akai held a certain respect for him since he had done everything he could to make up for the Achebes' issues, kept his word, and followed through with his promises in a timely manner. So, when Josh asked Akai if he could meet, Akai agreed to a quick meeting that afternoon, which Josh immediately leapt on.

HOWEVER, IF HE DID COME BACK, WE WOULD MAKE SURE THEY WERE TREATED **AS THOUGH THEY WERE PHOSSIUM'S ONE AND ONLY CLIENT.**

In the fifteen minutes Akai gave him, Josh explained everything that was happening at Phossium. Carolyn, he explained, didn't believe in giving excuses and neither did he, and her dedication to fixing the problems at the company was unshakable. He told Akai that ever since she'd started as CEO only a few months ago, she'd made significant changes, and he knew for a fact that she was currently addressing every one of the issues Akai had listed during his meeting with her, even though she thought she'd lost him as a customer.

"I told him that you're the real deal, that you meant it when you said that you were taking personal responsibility for fixing all of their account's problems, and that you were good to your word that those issues would never happen again," he said. "And even if his company didn't come back, I told him we were making serious improvements across the board. However, if he did come back, we would make sure that they were treated as though they were Phossium's one and only client, that their work product would be better than they could get anywhere else in the world, and that you would personally ensure the quality of their results."

He paused for a moment, then said, "I hope I didn't overstep my bounds in saying that, but I was pretty sure that's what you would have told him yourself, if he'd given you the time."

Carolyn nodded, still slightly numb with shock. "Of course, I would—I will—personally ensure that they're taken care of and that they receive nothing but our best work. But how did this go from that talk to this?" she said, holding up the work order.

"Well," said Josh, "after we spoke, Akai apparently had a meeting with his dad, during which he brought up both of our conversations with him. He said usually his dad doesn't believe in second chances, but because they'd been clients for so long and because Akai seemed to believe that we're genuine in our promises to make things right, he agreed to give us one last opportunity. So, this morning, Akai called me as I was getting ready for work and asked if I could swing by and pick this up."

Carolyn looked down at the order again and forced herself to believe what she was reading. It was a processing request for a class action that, once they got rolling on it, would comprise nearly a quarter of their current total production.

"I truly don't know what to say," she said to Josh. "This is amazing!"

She flipped through the small packet again and then with a start said, "I have to call them! Josh, I can't tell you enough how incredible this is. You have gone so far above and beyond, I don't even think it's measurable. I have to call Mr. Achebe now and confirm that we're moving on this immediately, but you and I need to talk soon. I need to find some way to thank you for standing up for what you believed and, in doing so, pretty much saving this company."

Josh rose from his seat and gave her another unabashed grin. "I only did what I thought was right—what I thought you would do in this situation. It's my honor. I hope the call goes well, and I'll be in touch," he said, and with that he walked out of the room.

Carolyn, phone receiver in hand, shook her head once again in astonishment, pulled the number for the Achebes out of her desk drawer, and made what she would soon consider to be the most rewarding phone call of her professional career.

CHAPTER 41
IN ALIGNMENT

aj and Batya couldn't believe their eyes, and even Walsh cracked one of his rare grins as she showed them the new work order from Achebe & Associates.

Raj, seated in one of the guest chairs, said with a grin, "We're going to need more people. Heck, we're going to need more machines!"

"Let's get through this work order first," Carolyn said somewhat firmly, reminding him that he still had almost an entire lower floor dedicated to document processing and several team members that were still in the process of embracing the new systems and culture.

He nodded. "Of course. Certainly. I'm just thinking ahead. I mean, if this is his test run with us, how big can these orders get?"

He rested his head on the back of the chair and stared thoughtfully at the ceiling.

"This is our defining moment," he said, half to himself and half to the room. Then he looked up and over at the other three. Batya nodded, while Walsh and Carolyn shared a quick look.

"THIS IS OUR DEFINING MOMENT," HE SAID, HALF TO HIMSELF AND HALF TO THE ROOM.

Walsh glanced at Carolyn again and then said, "I think we need to have a talk." And for the first time, Carolyn believed she knew what he was thinking.

Somewhat to her surprise, she was right.

"Despite how bad everything looked not that long ago, it seems like we might actually make something out of this company again," Walsh began. "But to do that, I think we need to make sure we're all on the same page. All of us," he said, looking at each of them. "Not just the four of us in this room or our immediate teams, but everyone in this company. We need to know that we're all 'in alignment,'" he cast a quick glance at Carolyn, "on how this organization works, how we plan to keep it working, where we intend to go with it, and that we're all in agreement on this culture we're trying to cultivate. If we can do that, then, well, we've definitely got something here."

"You're right," said Raj. "Like you just said, Mrs. Qualey, more than half of my team is still a little wary about getting on board with this culture of integrity and alignment. They've heard us talking about it in our own presentations and meetings, but they haven't quite embraced it yet."

Batya agreed. "It's the same with customer relations. I have a lot of people on board, but not everyone sees the benefit of it, and some don't really even understand it."

"I hear you," said Carolyn, "and it's certainly something that needs to happen, but the board meeting is tomorrow. How are we going to show them that we're a unified team when we still haven't held a meeting as an entire, unified team? There's no way we can pull it together today, and the board meeting is first thing tomorrow morning."

Walsh looked thoughtful for a moment and then said, "You were planning to address all the things I just said in your presentation, right?"

Carolyn nodded.

"Then let me take care of it," he said. Then, with a quick glance at his watch, he added, "Great news today, but I have some things I need to get to. Carolyn, I'll see you tomorrow, and Batya—I'm going to need you in about an hour. Can you swing by my office?"

Batya nodded, and Raj gave her a quizzical look, which she returned with a baffled expression that clearly said, *I have no idea what he's thinking*.

Carolyn, too, was perplexed, but trusted that Walsh knew what he was doing. In any case, her sole focus for the rest of the day and tomorrow was to show the board how far they'd come and hope that the next day wasn't her last.

Walsh left with a nod to the three of them, and the other two left Carolyn with words of encouragement, both telling her how great she was going to do tomorrow.

"They'll never know what hit them," said Batya, smiling.

Carolyn smiled and thanked them, though she couldn't help thinking, *I hope it's enough*.

CHAPTER 42
DAYBREAK

Carolyn barely slept that night. David kept her company for a while, sitting across from her at the dining room table and catching up on some of his work while she hammered away at her laptop. Occasionally, he'd get up and get her a fresh glass of water and, at one point, a hot chocolate made with her favorite cocoa.

By eleven o'clock, however, he decided to call it a night, kissed the top of her head, and told her not to stay up too late. Carolyn nodded and mumbled something in reply, so deep in her presentation for the quarterly board meeting that she didn't hear him go upstairs or close the bedroom door.

It was almost 2 a.m. by the time she pulled herself away, and even then, in the dark of her room with David gently snoring beside her, sleep remained elusive.

She must have slept at some point, however, because suddenly the gray light of dawn was seeping through the bedroom window, and her phone was chiming 5:30 a.m.

She thumbed the alarm off and stared for a moment at the shadowy ceiling, gathering her thoughts. David was still fast asleep—he wouldn't wake up for another hour at least—so she quietly rolled out of bed, slipped on her running clothes, and took off for a jog.

The cool morning air was exactly what she needed to wake her up. Her path led her around the neighborhood, down a connecting street, and by a tributary of the large river that ran through her city. She'd fiddled around with some of her workout music collections, but in the end, she opted for her audiobook of *Moby Dick* and was glad she had.

As the narrator regaled her with descriptions of glorious sunrises reflecting across miles of open sea, the sweet, salt air and the atmosphere of there being nothing to do but keep up the ship until the distant hiss of a whale pod called the crew to action, she lost herself in the story, imagining that the sunrise breaking across her own sky was the same as the sailors'; that she was perched, like them, in the cradle of a crow's nest, master of the sea, and yet as subject to its whims as a leaf on the surface of a pond. It was liberating and frightening at the same time, and it perfectly described how she felt that morning: like a small ship ready to take on a whale.

Back home, she quickly showered, dressed in the pencil skirt and blouse she'd laid out the night before, and read through a printout of her presentation one more time as she leaned against the kitchen island, eating a breakfast bar and sipping a hot cup of coffee.

Just as she finished, David walked in, hair mussed and still in his pajamas. He gave her a bleary-eyed grin, kissed her cheek, and ambled over to the coffee maker.

She smiled at him, scribbled a final note onto her printout, and tucked it into the bag already on her shoulder.

David raised an eyebrow over his coffee cup.

"You out?" he asked, glancing at the wall clock. Carolyn nodded.

"Yup, the meeting is being held in the corporate office across town, and I want to make sure I have everything I need to set up. I do not need any surprises today," she said, scooping up her car keys and doing one last check of herself in the hallway mirror. David walked up behind her and wrapped his arms around her waist. "You look great," he said, smiling. "And you're going to amaze them. Even that Dolores won't know what to do with herself."

Carolyn smiled, turned, and gave him a kiss. "Thank you, Hon. No matter what happens, I'll be happy when today is over."

She kissed him once more on the cheek, affectionately mussed his hair even more, and waved goodbye. He stood in the doorway, smiling, and giving her a thumbs-up as she drove away.

YOUR
CHANCES OF
GETTING WHAT
YOU WANT GO UP
**THE CLEARER
YOU ARE ABOUT
WHAT YOU WANT.**

CHAPTER 43
SUPPOSITIONS

The headquarters of Algus Consolidated Systems was a looming twenty-two-story steel-and-glass structure that glinted like a star in the early morning light. Carolyn could see it flickering brightly as she crossed the downtown river bridge, even though she was still miles away.

Thankfully, traffic was light, and it was still a good hour and a half before the board meeting began when she arrived at Algus's glass tower and checked in. The assistant at the front desk eyed her coldly and asked for her ID, then made her stand in front of a small desk camera to have her picture taken for a temporary visitor badge. Despite having her driver's license right in front of her, the woman still spelled Carolyn's name wrong—Caroline Quailey—but Carolyn just shrugged it off and clipped the tag to her lapel. She had bigger concerns today.

The assistant directed her to a room on the top floor, and after taking a minute to adjust the extra AV equipment bag she'd brought with her, Carolyn walked down the foyer's wide, marble hallway to one of the stainless-steel elevators and waited for the next lift.

When it arrived, she took a step forward and almost stumbled over her own feet in shock.

Standing in the elevator was Raj, coffee cup in hand and looking as surprised as she felt. He choked down the sip of coffee he'd just taken and, eyes watering, managed to work out a, "Hi, Mrs. Qualey."

"Hello, Raj," she managed to reply as she stepped into the elevator, looking at him with an eyebrow arched in question. Raj glanced at the closing elevator door and then, as the panels gently hissed shut, he shrugged and looked over at her.

"Well, guess I'll go ahead and take you upstairs, since you're here," he said, pressing the "22" button.

Carolyn nodded, but she wasn't about to leave the giant question still hanging in the air.

"Raj, what in heaven's name are you doing here?" she asked.

Raj looked down at the floor and blushed. "Just, well . . . we all know how important today is for you, and I wanted to make sure you have everything you need. The AV setup can be difficult no matter where you are, and since I wasn't sure if they had anyone here who could help—or if they would even offer to have someone help you set up—I figured I'd get here early and make sure there weren't any surprises," he said, finally looking up at her.

Carolyn smiled. "Thank you, Raj. For a second there, I thought Algus might have been the company that was trying to recruit you."

Raj laughed and shook his head vigorously. "Ha! Not a chance. Really, I just wanted to make sure you were set for success. I

INTELLIGENCE IS A GIFT.
PERSISTENCE IS A VIRTUE.

mean, it's no secret around the office how Dolores Pendergrast has been treating you recently," he said.

Carolyn's eyes widened in surprise. She thought she'd kept that last encounter out of the public eye, but then again, she was still having a hard time getting Bridget to understand the importance of not gossiping.

"Well, thank you for the thought, but I'm sure I can handle it," she said, patting the bag of AV equipment with her. "And I can also handle Dolores. She's a lot more bark than bite."

Raj nodded. "All the same, I'm glad I stopped by. Wait 'til you see this setup . . . ."

As though on cue, the elevator door slid open, and Carolyn and Raj stepped into a marble-floored hallway with massive original works of art interspersed along its length, all professionally lit with bronze gallery lights, and living plants blossoming out of antique jars set on post-modern steel stands that tastefully lined the hallway.

Raj directed her to the left, down a long hallway to a double glass door, which he held open for her as she walked in.

The room was Carolyn's second shock for the morning.

It was massive. The ceiling was at least twenty feet high, and the floor-to-ceiling windows along one entire side gave her a breathtaking view of the city. In the distance, she could see the glint of the river and the bridge she'd driven over only half an hour ago. Heavy drapes filled the corners of the room, and she could see a switch that would automatically close them over the windows, which came in handy if one needed to use the gigantic television screen suspended against the room's far wall.

She was still taking it all in when she felt Raj lifting the heavy bags from her shoulders. She looked over at him, and he grinned at her awed expression. "Yeah, it's a pretty nice room, isn't it?" he said.

"I'll say," she said. Her little AV bag suddenly seemed like a joke as she looked at the giant TV screen with no obvious inputs. Raj walked over and pressed his hand against the wooden wall, which silently swung open to reveal a control panel that would have looked just at home at NASA as it did in the conference room. He pressed a few buttons, then walked back to the table, flicked Carolyn's laptop on, and began entering data. After about a minute, the giant screen came to life, and the Power-Point she'd created appeared, the words almost a foot high on a background that seemed at least as tall as she was.

"Raj?" she said, staring up at the giant screen.

"Yes, Mrs. Qualey?" he said as he typed the few last commands into the computer.

"I'm glad you're here," she said.

He laughed gently. "I'm glad I could help," he said, clicking a final button, checking his watch one last time, and stepping away.

Raj walked her through launching the program, making sure she knew what to click and when, and then reconfirmed with her when she would be giving her presentation. "Just so we can be rooting for you," he said with a smile.

"Thank you so much," she said, handing him the little AV bag. "Think you could take this back to the office for me? I don't want them to think I'm some kind of luddite."

He laughed and took the bag, wished her luck once again, and left her to it.

Carolyn had run through her notes so many times that she probably could have given her presentation backward, but she ran through it one more time, to be sure. Just as she clicked to the last slide, the door swung open . . . and Carolyn froze.

Dolores came strutting into the room, a dark beauty in the most professional outfit Carolyn had ever seen her wear. Her hair was pulled up in a simple-yet-elegant topknot and she was wearing, for the first time in Carolyn's memory, a pair of wireframe glasses.

She glanced at Carolyn without expression, assessed the rest of the room in a glance, and then looked back over her shoulder at the man holding the door open for her.

"Bob, be a dear and bring in my things," she said.

For the first time, Carolyn noticed the man standing behind Dolores. His suit was slightly wrinkled, the collar a size too tight—as were the pants—and his thinning hair fell in unkempt strands around his ruddy face. It was Bob Quills, Phossium's former director of document processing.

Quills nodded at Dolores and picked up the two black bags on the floor just outside the conference room doors. He glanced at Carolyn as he walked in with them, giving her a sour smirk as he passed her, and placed Dolores's bags on the table.

Dolores reached in and pulled out a stack of neat, black, matte folders with the words "Phossium Enterprises" embossed in a flourish of gold script on the front.

"Pass these around, would you, Bob?" she said.

Quills immediately began pulling stacks of folders out of the bags and placing them in front of the chairs.

"Don't forget the pens," she added.

Quills nodded, shaking his head at his forgetfulness, and pulled a bag of gold-and-black fountain pens from the bag, placing them neatly next to each folder.

Dolores watched Quills, her back turned to Carolyn, until Quills was done. It was only when he was finally finished and looking at Dolores expectantly that Dolores turned and acknowledged Carolyn.

"I see you're giving a PowerPoint," said Dolores, glancing at the screen. "It's been a while since we've seen one of those. It'll be just like high school," she smiled.

"Good morning, Dolores," said Carolyn. "I see you have a presentation, as well."

"I do," she said. "Of course I do. I need to be ready to step in when the board realizes that they need to find someone to fill the CEO role at Phossium."

Carolyn arched an eyebrow at her. "Oh?"

"My dear, you didn't think this was going to be a real chance to save your job, did you? Why, Bert even asked me to have something ready, just in case. Truly, I don't think a single person on this board has any confidence left in you. They've seen the numbers; they know how much money you're losing. To be honest, I'm surprised they're even giving you a chance to speak."

Dolores glared coldly at Carolyn. "In my opinion," she said, "this meeting is more an excess of kindness than anything else; a chance to share your last words."

Instead of responding, Carolyn simply stepped away from Dolores, picked up one of the folders on the table, and flipped it open.

There, on the cover page, was the same name, "Phossium Enterprises," in the same script, but this time with the words "Dolores Pendergrast, CEO" and "Robert Quills, Executive Vice President" inscribed beneath it.

She thumbed through the pages. The first several were all charts of Phossium's financial progress—if you could call it that—from the day Algus purchased it until the beginning of last month. The downward trend was obvious, and it wasn't unfamiliar to Carolyn. She knew this was going to be one of the main questions on everyone's mind. But there was a lot Dolores didn't know about, including the Achebe account.

A few pages later revealed a new organizational chart, again showing Dolores in the CEO chair and Quills directly underneath her. Carolyn was surprised to see several names of people who had either quit or been fired in the directorial—and various other—positions. The next page began an overview of Dolores's "recovery" plan, which included a drastic slashing of pay and benefits across the board, her full list of firings, and finally, plans to outsource the vast majority of document processing to a facility that Carolyn was familiar with—a high-volume processing company outside the country that was known for mediocre results and less-than-helpful customer service. They were fast, but that was about it, and they offered none of the additional custom services that Carolyn and the others had been developing. The last few pages were financial projections, with attractive-looking upward climbs in pleasing green and black colors.

Carolyn looked up, expecting to see Dolores staring at her smugly, but instead she was across the room, opening the door for Wagner and two other board members who had just arrived. Carolyn quickly placed the folder back on the table and was about to walk over when she saw Quills watching her from the other side of the table. He smiled grimly at her.

"It will be nice to have things back the way they were again," he said, nodding at the folder.

Carolyn shook her head. "No, it won't, Bob. And it's not going to happen. I don't know how you two got it in your heads that you were going to run Phossium, but Dolores has no sense of how to actually run a business—all she knows are numbers. And on top of that, she can't be trusted. She'll throw you under the bus before she gets a drop of mud on those fancy heels of hers."

Quills slowly waved one chubby index finger in the air at her. "Tut, tut, Mrs. Qualey. Jealously gets you nowhere. Dolores knows exactly how to run a business, and it starts with cutting out all that extra fat you seem to enjoy cultivating. Plus, she obviously knows a quality business mind when she sees one, which is why she's making me her VP."

Suddenly, Dolores's voice piped up from across the room, "Bob, dear, would you run downstairs and let the coffee service know we're ready for them?"

Quills gave Carolyn a contemptuous smile and half-trotted across the room. "Of course, Ms. Pendergrast," he said, ducking out and nodding in greeting to the board members. "Right away," he added, disappearing down the hall.

"More like her service dog," Carolyn muttered under her breath, watching as Quills practically scampered down the marble corridor.

For a quick moment, she closed her eyes, took a deep breath, and concentrated on breathing compassion in and breathing frustration out. After a handful of breaths, she opened her eyes, allowed a soft smile to settle on her lips, and walked over to greet the arriving board members.

CHAPTER 44

THE BOARD MEETING

n typical fashion, Wagner began the meeting promptly at 9:00 a.m., despite a few of the board members running a bit late. The agenda for the day was heavy, with status reports from more than two dozen different organizations being presented just before lunch. Carolyn listened to all of them with fascination, amazed, as she always was, at the scope of businesses that Algus oversaw and with what precision they conducted their operations. She knew that Phossium was ultimately part of a much larger conglomeration of businesses, and it was good to be reminded of just how far that network stretched.

As the lunch hour approached, Carolyn began to feel the old rush of adrenaline and anxiety that she always felt before speaking in public. She was scheduled to give her presentation immediately after lunch, and Wagner was moving the meeting along right on time. At noon, precisely, he called a break, and a local catering company wheeled in lunch.

Too keyed up to eat a full meal, she grabbed a light salad and talked with some of the board members seated near her during the break. Occasionally she looked up at Dolores, seated as close to Wagner as she could get, and watched her alternately

fawning over him and speaking in short, sharp sentences to Quills, who took it all with unshakable devotion.

Carolyn shook her head. Dolores was Dolores, and over the past several weeks, Carolyn had decided that the best way to deal with her was to ignore her completely, even though she was doing her best to rattle her cage at today's meeting. Carolyn's team had done some truly incredible work over the past month, and if what she had to say to the board didn't blow them out of the water, then she truly didn't deserve her job.

At 1:20 p.m., the catering service cleared their plates and whisked out of the room, the only evidence they'd been there the lingering smell of after-lunch coffee. Exactly ten minutes later, Wagner called the meeting to order and welcomed Carolyn to the front of the room.

"Mrs. Qualey, as you all remember, has been the chief executive officer for one of our more recent acquisitions, Phossium Enterprises," said Wagner to the rest of the board. "We all knew the business was going to be a challenge when we acquired it, and today Mrs. Qualey will share with us how it is progressing. Mrs. Qualey, if you will?"

Wagner gestured for her to take the floor as he took his seat. Carolyn, already standing, smiled and nodded, then walked to the front of the table so she could stand in front of the enormous screen. She flicked her computer on and clicked the buttons that Raj told her to press and then gave an audible gasp of surprise . . . along with the rest of the room.

There on the screen of her computer and on the giant screen behind her was the entire staff of Phossium, gathered in the lunch hall where she'd given her integrity presentation not so long ago. The room was completely quiet as more than a hundred pairs of eyes stared back at her expectantly. Then, the screen shook slightly, and Walsh suddenly appeared at the front of the crowd, waving at her with a smile on his face.

"Good afternoon, Carolyn!" he said, and the rest of Phossium waved and smiled at her from behind him.

Not knowing what else to do, she smiled and waved back.

"Hope this isn't too much of a shock, but we did want to surprise you," he said, and with a quick look from side to side, Batya, Raj, and Josh stepped into the screen to stand beside him.

"We all know how important it is to you that everyone here be on the same page, so instead of making you give your speech twice, I asked Raj to set this up," said Walsh.

Raj waved at Carolyn, who rolled her eyes and smiled at him.

"So, we're ready when you are!" Walsh said. "Just remember to watch the camera on your laptop so we can see you, and click that button Raj showed you to make the presentation appear. Don't worry, you won't see us, but we'll still see you, and we'll hear it all," he said.

Carolyn looked down at her laptop camera and gave Walsh a smile and a thumbs-up, and instantly the entire crowd at Phossium burst into applause. Walsh, Batya, Josh, and Raj all joined in, and suddenly, Carolyn felt a completely unexpected surge of confidence. Here she was, in front of the board, and she literally had her entire company behind her, supporting her. It was amazing!

"Thank you, Mr. Walsh, and thank you, everyone," she said and looked up to see all of the board members—apart from Dolores and Quills—smiling back at her.

"This was obviously completely unexpected, but I'm so glad to have my entire team here with me today. We've come a long way over the past several months, and every single person in that room at Phossium has played an important part in that progress," she said, then clicked the last two buttons that Raj had shown her, and the familiar presentation appeared on the screen.

"Whew! I'm glad that worked," she said, grinning. "Now, before we dive into the present, let's take a quick look at where we've been."

With that, Carolyn shared a compressed version of her presentation on integrity and the importance of being intentional and persistent about it, sharing this vital foundation now not only with the people in the room in front of her but with every last Phossium team member.

From there, she moved on to feedback and explained how she encouraged her team members to stand up for integrity by holding each other accountable for any breaches of that value, speaking to one another in a way that reminded them that they held great respect for each other, and calling out breaches in order to encourage each other to be better—to be their best selves—and that they expected that person to do the same for them.

That interaction, she explained, also played to their methods of conversing and social contracting—in other words, the way they were expected to speak to each other and, just as importantly, to listen to each other. Commands, for instance, were simply a way to ensure that an action took place, and requests were used to give the other person the option of saying "no" if they needed to defend a previous "yes" to another task.

Clarity, too, was vital to an organization that functioned with integrity, as miscommunication could cause instant upset on every level of the organization. For that reason, she explained, she also encouraged team members to speak as much as possible based on fact, instead of simply sharing their beliefs or, worse, stories. She told the board about Walsh's discovery of this quality and how identifying the different ways that their customers spoke led them not only to discover new ways to improve their services but to improve their conversations between each other, as well.

"For any system to work with integrity—which, by definition, is 'soundness; an unimpaired condition, and completeness; the quality or state of being complete or undivided'—each part must understand exactly what is needed from the other part," Carolyn explained. "The more unified the system, the more efficiently and effectively we can do our work. And every one of us understands that to impact something in one part of the business is to impact every part of the business. 'Whatever affects one directly, affects all indirectly,' as Martin Luther King Jr. once said[3]. And since there is no 'over there'—no task within the company that doesn't affect the entire company on some level—we also encourage each other to think of any 'problems' we run into not as 'problems' but as 'possibilities.' What's possible here? And how can we use it to think outside the box?"

It was this understanding, she explained, of how interconnected and interdependent each part of Phossium was to the others, that led them to the creation of several of the ideas they were exploring to more fully provide the best service possible to their customers. In one sense, she said, the customer stood on both ends of the smoothly functioning mechanism they called Phossium; the customer gave the work order that started the mechanism moving—and the mechanism functioned for the sole purpose of providing the final work product to the customer as optimally and efficiently as possible at the end.

3   Source: http://www2.oberlin.edu/external/EOG/BlackHistoryMonth/MLK/CommAddress.html

"In the end, it's the customers who pay our bills," she explained, "and by making them the objective of our culture—in understanding that we needed to have integrity to work together to turn out the best results for our customers—we gave our culture even more strength: We gave it intention and purpose. That is where our power comes from—not from pleasing our team members or our peers or even our higher-ups, but from understanding and pleasing our *customers*."

Next, Carolyn flipped to a slide that read "Four Conversations."

"Now, for everyone in our organization to be in alignment with each other, I want everyone in this room and at Phossium to understand four things: how this organization works; how we plan to keep it working; where we intend to go with it; and confirming that we're all in agreement on what we need to do to sustain our culture."

With that, Carolyn walked the board—and all of Phossium—through four sets of questions and answers, each geared toward aligning the company on its perspective, intent, actions, and culture, and shared a variety of models on each to demonstrate how they planned to accomplish all four objectives.

Only as she wrapped up her explanation on the last slide did Carolyn realize she only had five minutes left, and yet she still had so much more to go through. For a split second, she considered rapid firing through the last dozen or so slides, but then she stopped and simply looked across the board room for a moment. Twenty-four pairs of eyes looked at her expectantly, and she chose to ignore the two that were glowering at her fiercely.

"You know what?" she said. "We're going to wrap this up just a little differently than I planned, but . . . this is better."

With that, Carolyn walked up to her laptop and clicked the command to switch views. Instantly, the entire screen was once again filled with the faces of Phossium.

"Guys, just so you know, you're on screen on this end now, as well," she said with a smile and wave. Dozens of people in the first several rows suddenly sat up a little straighter, and a few gave her a small wave back. Batya, Raj, Josh, and Walsh just smiled back at her encouragingly.

Carolyn turned her focus back to the board.

"I want you to see my team as I share this last part with you," she said. "Because it's important to me that they understand how incredibly valuable every one of them is to this company.

"What they've done so far has taken an incredible amount of courage. When I first walked into this company, I thought that there was no way I could turn it around—that it was stuck in this dark place, where no one wanted to speak to each other and preferred to gossip behind one another's backs—where no one wanted to extend themselves to anyone else or provide any extra help beyond what was absolutely required of them. It felt like no one cared, and no one wanted to care. I thought I was

completely alone, and every time I reached out, it was like hitting my head against a brick wall.

"But then I discovered a way to look at what Phossium had become from a different perspective—to see the issue not as an impenetrable wall but as simply an *absence* of anyone standing for something greater. So, I looked again and suddenly, I began to find some bright spots."

She gestured toward the screen. "Batya there was my first lit match in the darkness, and then Raj. Then, unbelievably, Hugh here, who has become my anchor to reality and my voice to those team members who have been around for years, some even decades. Josh, too, has recently been an amazing example of what it truly means to have moral courage.

"Over the past few months, I and several of these team members have gone to the others in Phossium. We've told them about all the things I've shared with you today: about integrity and interconnectedness and possibility and feedback. All these, and other wonderful things we've discovered along the way as we worked to make the mechanism we call Phossium function wholly and completely, create an environment in which we know, without the slightest doubt in our minds, that we can truly, entirely trust one another . . . and do what we say we're going to do—intentionally and always.

"To do this, to stand for this kind of culture, took enormous courage. If you say to someone, for instance, 'I expect better from you, because I know you're capable of more,' you're not going to get a smile and a handshake. People bite back. People get angry, and standing for integrity not only in your own actions, but also in expecting it from others, is monumentally hard. But they've done it," said Carolyn, who now shifted her gaze to Dolores and Quills. "They did it, knowing that there would still be some people who resisted them, who would always try to let the darkness back in and extinguish their efforts, preferring the way 'things used to be' instead of seeing the potential in something better. They chose to have moral courage, and, in doing so, they burned away more of the darkness in a matter of months than I could have done alone in a lifetime."

She turned to the camera and looked at every face in the gathered crowd at Phossium.

"Thank you," she said. "From the bottom of my heart, thank you. Thank you for believing in this company, for believing in integrity, in trust, in our customers—and for believing in me and in each other. You are all amazing, and I can't wait to see what noble and mighty things we'll be able to accomplish together."

Then she turned back to the boardroom. "And those accomplishments have already started." She quickly turned her presentation back on and flicked quickly down to the last slide, which simply showed one figure.

"Because of our efforts, both in reaching out to our customers and in generating a peak performance culture, this number represents the profit—not gross income, but profit—we are contracted to make from a single account. This customer believes in our system, thanks to the efforts of this incredible team. Should this order turn out successfully—and it will—they plan to increase this number by at least ten-fold, putting us not only back in the black, but on the fast track for expansion." Then she switched the screen one last time and turned her eyes back to Phossium. "Because of you," she said, "this became possible."

BECAUSE OF OUR EFFORTS, BOTH IN REACHING OUT TO OUR CUSTOMERS AND IN GENERATING A PEAK PERFORMANCE CULTURE,

THIS NUMBER REPRESENTS PROFIT—NOT GROSS INCOME, BUT PROFIT.

The crowd at Phossium, larger than life on the big screen in front of the entire board, suddenly burst into a cacophony of clapping and cheers, hoots and hollers. Batya, Josh, and Raj gave their own "whoops" of joy, and Walsh rose to his feet, clapping and smiling.

The board couldn't help but be swept up in the excitement, applauding heartily and congratulating Carolyn.

She felt herself blushing and didn't care. She nodded deeply and then gestured toward the screen to include the entirety of Phossium in receiving their applause. Finally, she turned to the camera and said, "Okay, team. I've got to go. Thank you so much for being here!" Those who heard her through the ebbing cheers waved goodbye as Raj gave her a thumbs-up and disappeared from the screen. A few seconds later the camera feed switched off and, once again, she was alone in the room with the board.

Only as she turned back to the room did she discover that Dolores was standing, and in her hands was her black and gold presentation, the front flipped open to an angry-looking chart.

"How can you all be applauding her?" she was saying, flicking a perfectly manicured hand in Carolyn's direction as though shooing a fly. "She's just playing to your emotions! There's no way that crowd on the screen was a 'surprise' to her; she planned all along to have all those people staring at us, guilting us into giving her another chance. She doesn't deserve another chance! Look at the numbers!" She said, shaking the chart angrily. "Don't you see? Carolyn Qualey's time at Phossium has resulted in nothing but massive losses for us and our shareholders. She's a failure! A complete and utter failure!"

Vagrant stands of hair had fallen in Dolores's eyes, and her skin was blotchy red with anger. Quills, sitting next to her, reached up and tried to calmly pat her arm.

"Don't try to calm me down, Bob. You've been against her from the very beginning. You know! You know exactly how bad she's been for this company. The numbers don't lie. She's done nothing but make things worse," she said, looking around the room. "She's manipulating you. This isn't success—we don't even know if that number up there is true. For all we know, she just made this figure up to save her job. It's nowhere in the financial reports, and, in fact, I have it on good word that the Achebes canceled their account almost two weeks ago."

Wagner, who had been watching Dolores with barely concealed surprise, turned to Carolyn. "She does make a valid point," he said. "I haven't heard anything about the Achebes' status, but the financial reports have not shown any growth. In fact, it's been a steady downward trend, and no one here heard about this new work order until just now."

Carolyn nodded and pulled a small stack of papers from her bag, which she handed to the person next to her and gestured for her to pass around.

"I'm glad you asked, Mr. Wagner," she said. "On this chart, you'll find the progress we've made over the past three weeks, including the number of current accounts that have renewed with us, as well as the one on the screen and the new accounts we've brought on thanks to a number of referrals, which are also listed. And attached to the last page, you'll find a certified copy of that work order from Mr. Achebe himself. I believe it should allay any concerns that this figure may be 'made up.'"

There was a quiet rustle as the papers made their way around the room, and Carolyn watched Wagner's eyebrows rise as he read through the report.

After a minute he said, "This is quite impressive, Mrs. Qualey." Then he turned to Dolores. "Ms. Pendergrast, does this answer your question satisfactorily?"

Dolores, jaw clenched, nodded sharply. "It does."

"Well, then," said Wagner, clapping his hands together. "I'd say it's been a rocky road, but it looks like you're turning this company around, Mrs. Qualey. Thank you so much for your hard work, and we look forward to hearing even more great news from you at our next quarterly meeting. Although, between you and me," he said with a wink, "let's try to keep the next report a little shorter and a lot less crowded, okay?"

Carolyn smiled. "Of course, Mr. Wagner," she said. "You have my word."

KEEPING LOVE ALIVE

**"Love is simply the name for the desire
and pursuit of the whole"**

ARISTOPHANES, "THE DIALOGUE RELATED BY
APOLLODORUS," FROM *THE SYMPOSIUM* BY PLATO

———

"**C**ome on, Mom! I'm sure you look great," said Gus as he picked at his tie in the hallway mirror. He glanced up the stairs and then looked over at his dad, who was sitting on the couch. David gave him a noncommittal shrug.

"What? I can't make her go any faster," he said.

Gus sighed and looked over at his sister and her husband, who were talking quietly on the bar stools at the open kitchen island. Sadie looked up at him. "What?" she said.

"Could you please go tell Mom to hurry up?" he said.

"Why? We're not running late," she said.

Gus rolled his eyes. "She's been up there for more than an hour. Knowing Mom, she's probably just running through her speech for the eightieth time when we could be hitting the road."

Sadie groaned. "Ugh, fine, *Dr.* Augustus."

She stood up, brushed the wrinkles out of the back of her dress, and kissed her husband on the cheek. "I'll be right back, Babe," she said. "Keep an eye on Lynn, would you?" He nodded and looked down at the tiny bundle in the car seat next to his stool. The infant's eyes were closed, and she was breathing deeply under her summer-weight blanket.

"I don't think she's going to budge for a while," he said with a tired smile.

Sadie nodded, then turned and walked up the stairs, glaring at Gus for making her get up.

Gus sat down on the couch next to his dad and sighed. David leaned over and gave him a fatherly pat on the knee.

"Don't worry, Doc, we'll get there in plenty of time. It's a big day for her," he said, always taking the opportunity to use his son's hard-earned title. "It's not every day you retire from being the CEO of a multinational company."

Upstairs, Sadie knocked gently on Carolyn's bedroom door.

"Mom?" she said.

"Come in, Hon," said Carolyn.

Sadie swung the door open and walked inside. Carolyn was staring in the bathroom mirror, tucking loose strands of her white-gray hair into an elegant up-do. She wore a pair of pearl earrings and a matching necklace, which in turn gave the rich, forest-green cocktail dress she was wearing a classic flair.

She looked beautiful and perfectly put together, but as Sadie got closer, she could see tears in her mom's eyes.

"Mom, are you okay?" she asked, placing a gentle hand on her back.

Carolyn nodded. "Of course, sweetheart, I'm fine. I just can't believe . . ." she looked at herself in the mirror again and dabbed a tissue under her eyes. " . . . I just can't believe today is finally here. I never really expected to retire, you know?"

She turned to her daughter with a smile and thought, perhaps for the billionth time, how beautiful she was. She wore her long, golden brown hair in a loose French braid and the cornflower blue of her cocktail dress perfectly matched her eyes—the same shade as her father's.

Sadie grinned and hugged Carolyn as hard as she could. "Mom, even though this is your 'retirement party,' I seriously doubt you're going to be completely out of their lives after today. You will find ways to help out, I'm sure. Whether they ask for it or not."

Carolyn laughed. "You're right, I know. It's just so incredible, how far we've come in such a short time." She took one last look at herself in the mirror, pressed her shoulders back and said, "Okay, let's go."

The entire Qualey family arrived at Phossium just before 6:00 p.m. As they walked in, Carolyn saw that the foyer lights were on but was surprised to see that there were barely any lights on in the lunchroom, where her retirement party was supposedly being held.

"Are we sure this is the right time, Gus?" she asked, glancing down at her watch.

He nodded. "Sure, I'm sure," he said. "And I'm sure there's a reason . . ." he said as he walked into the room ahead of her, at which point the lights instantly came on and Carolyn, who was walking immediately behind Gus, ran right into his back.

A resounding roar of applause suddenly filled the room, and somewhere behind all the people, a jazz band kicked in with an upbeat rendition of "For He's a Jolly Good Fellow."

Carolyn looked around in shock. Not only was the entire Phossium crew from main headquarters there, but most of the people from their California branch, their Virginia branch, and even their London and Dublin branches were there, all of them cheering and clapping for her as she and her family walked into the room.

She clasped her hands in front of her, smiling from ear to ear and unashamed of the tears rolling liberally down her cheeks. This was her family, both standing there with her and filling the old lunchroom to the gills, and the mixture of pride and joy and loss

that suddenly came rushing through her was almost more than she could stand.

And there, at the front of the crowd, was Walsh, smiling with that easy grin he'd become known for over the years and looking fifteen years younger than the day she'd met him. He embraced Carolyn as the cheering began to calm down and people began lining up to congratulate her. "Can't believe it's finally today, huh?" he said with a smile. She nodded fiercely, doing her best to wipe away the tears.

"Ah, you're not going too far. I'm sure we'll still see you around; you don't let go of anything very easily," he said smiling and gave her another hug.

She laughed, hugged him back, and playfully socked him in the arm. When she looked up again, she was pleased to see Raj and Batya standing there, both of them with their respective families. Batya had brought her husband with her, as well as her three-year-old daughter, Abby; and Raj had his wife and three young boys with him: Sa'id, Ramez, and Cyrus, ages six, four, and three, respectively. The moment she turned toward them, the boys ran up to her and hugged her at varying heights, shouting, "Congratulations, Aunt Lynnie!" Little Abby joined in as well, and both Batya and Raj laughed at the stacks of children around her legs.

Carolyn bent down and hugged each of them in return, then hugged Raj and Batya for all they were worth, followed by their spouses. She was amazed by how much they'd all grown over the years, both personally and together. Raj was now head of document processing across the entire organization, and Batya had just accepted the position of chief operations officer. They were both excelling in their roles, and Carolyn couldn't have been prouder.

Just as she was about to turn around, another familiar face appeared in front of her. It was Josh, smiling and looking exactly the same as he did ten years ago, except for a little bit of salt to his dark hair. He'd risen rapidly at the company since the day he saved the Achebe account, and today, he held down the role of European director. It was because of him that they now had two international offices and planned to open two more soon.

He reached out and gave her a big hug, which she returned happily. "We've come a long way, haven't we?" he said.

She nodded. "Thanks to you," she said. "Thanks to everyone here, but especially you. You're going to do more great things with this company than I ever imagined, I'm sure of it."

He smiled and gave her one last big hug before she was swept away by yet another familiar face, wrapped in another warm hug, and reminded of past adventures and escapades throughout the incredibly memorable last ten years—all while her immediate family looked on with pride.

It was almost half an hour after she walked in when the sound of a glass being tink-tink-tinked with a piece of cutlery could be heard over the microphone at the front of the room.

The crowd gradually quieted down as all eyes turned to the stage, where Hugh Walsh stood with champagne glass in hand.

"Carolyn?" he said, looking around the room for her. "Would the guest of honor please come to the stage?"

Carolyn emerged from the crowd, dozens of hands reaching out to pat her on the back as she walked by, and she took her place next to Hugh. Carolyn looked radiant, the only sign of the past ten years in the color of her hair, which she'd finally allowed to go gray. She was still trim, still vibrant, and didn't look even close to the seventy-three years she now boasted.

Hugh turned to the small table set behind him and picked up a second champagne glass, which he placed in her hands. She smiled and mouthed "Thank you."

"You're welcome," said Hugh into the microphone and then turned to the crowd. "Now, I know this is the point where we all start shouting 'speech!' and demand a whole liturgy of elegant and timeless words from our fearless leader, but I have the mike right now, and I'm going to use it."

He cleared his throat, adjusted his tie a little, and then proffered the glass in his hand toward Carolyn.

"Ten years ago, this fiery upstart of a woman burst into the perfectly comfortable bubble I'd made of my life here at Phossium and turned it completely upside down. And I can't say I was pleased with her about it," he said to a wave of giggles and laughter around the room.

"But what I can say is that she grew on me. As much as I'd come to hate the idea of change, I could see that this firebrand had

some pretty good ideas, and she wasn't going to let a grouchy old codger like me stand in her way. So she kept pursuing that ideal despite me, and, like it or not, I began to see some incredible changes take place in this company."

He smiled and looked around at the crowded room. "A lot of you don't remember what it was like here at Phossium some ten, eleven years ago, but I'll be the first one to tell you that it wasn't pretty. We didn't work well together, we siloed ourselves in our offices and departments, and we put out a work product that, to be honest, sucked. Sorry for the language, kids," he added quickly, looking over at Batya and Raj, both of whom just rolled their eyes at him and smiled.

"It was Carolyn here who first introduced the culture that we all know and love today. Because of her, we have some of the best people in the industry working here and a work environment that is envied around the world. We have a reputation of excellence, and because of that, we're able to bring on the best clients and work on the best projects. We've made our industry into a true art form—a feat which wouldn't have been possible if we hadn't started with the right foundation by learning the value of integrity and the incredible value of trusting in each other.

"Therefore, it is with great pride, but also a great sense of loss, that I thank Carolyn today for the decade of service she gave to this organization; for the heart and warmth and love that she poured into it every day, along with all the blood, sweat, and tears. She wasn't above a single task, and she was always willing to help another in need. She was a true role model, and many of us, myself included, will thank our lucky stars if one day we turn out to be half the person she is. Carolyn—to you," he said, raising his glass higher and toward the room, and with a rustling of movement, the entire crowd raised their glasses, as well.

"Thank you for your unflinching stand for integrity and for demanding only the best from us, because you believed in us even more than we believed in ourselves. Thank you for seeing greatness in us, and standing by us until we saw it for ourselves. And thank you for your leadership, for your strength, and for your love. Heck, just thank you for being you," he said. "Cheers!"

And with a thunderous roar, the crowd joined in a collective "Cheers!" as Hugh reached down and wrapped Carolyn up in his arms. Carolyn squeezed him back as hard as she could, tears once again rolling down her cheeks. "You're too much, Hugh, too much," she said, laughing.

"No, you are, Carolyn," he said, smiling. "No one could ever fill the shoes you're leaving behind. We'll miss you more than you'll ever know."

She hugged him one last time and kissed him on the cheek, then wiped at her tears as he tried to hand her the microphone. For a moment, she tried to brush it away, but neither Hugh nor the crowd would have it.

"Speech! Speech! Speech!" someone started chanting in the crowd, and the whole room quickly joined in. Finally, Carolyn took the microphone out of Hugh's hands and waved the crowd down, still wiping tears from her eyes.

"Okay, alright, my goodness you're a strong-willed crew. Who trained you?" she asked with a smile, which caused a wave of laughter to ripple through the crowd.

"It's going to be impossible to follow up on Hugh's incredible words, but I'll give it a shot."

She cleared her throat and looked down for a minute, then looked out across the gathered crowd, eyes shining.

"When I accepted the job of CEO at Phossium, I had no idea what I was getting myself into. At the time, I simply knew that I wanted to run a company, and it didn't really matter to me what company that was. I was hungry for leadership, and I came charging into this company like a bull into the ring . . . and was immediately kicked in the teeth. Figuratively, of course," she said, to a murmur of laughter.

"But the reality was that I felt helpless. The environment here was so dark and the work product so poor that I was convinced there was no way it could be turned around. I almost listened to those who kept telling me I couldn't do it, that I wouldn't be able to change anything. But in the middle of that helplessness, just when I'd almost decided to throw in the towel, I found this."

Carolyn reached into the small clutch tucked under her arm and pulled out a frail piece of paper.

"To this day, I still don't know who wrote this down, but this parable gave me the strength to see what was possible—to know that even unimaginable darkness can be turned away by the light of a single match," and, with that, Carolyn read, for the first time in ten years, the Parable of the Match in the Root Cellar.

Of all the people in the room, only a handful had heard the story—including Hugh, Raj, and Batya. And as she read, not a single one of them tried to fight back the tears. It was because of this deceptively simplistic tale that Carolyn had sought them out, forced them to see the environment they were allowing themselves to live in, and driven them to find the strength to demand better.

" . . . The light spits and flares, breathlessly gutters, then holds its flame just as you open the box," Carolyn read from the delicate page. "As you do, the darkness that pours from under the lid engulfs the room and completely extinguishes the flame. Dear reader, is this how darkness works?" She looked around the room as she asked the question.

"Of course not," she continued. "Darkness is not the opposite of light—it is the absence of it. And the smallest flicker of the thinnest flame, all on its own, can overpower the most infinite night."

After reading the last line, Carolyn paused a moment, letting the silence fill the room, then she carefully folded the paper and pressed it against her heart.

"Every one of you gathered here today is a match. You wouldn't be here if you didn't believe that your word is the only thing that you truly have to give, and that standing by it is your greatest responsibility. Each of you burns with this passion, and you spread it wherever you go. You rely on each other to do the same, and because we have proven to each other that we can be relied on to stand by our word, to have integrity, to imme-diately acknowledge if we fail to stand by it for any reason, we have incredible trust in each other. And it's this trust that has allowed us to become, quite literally, one of the top document-processing companies in the world.

"Because of you, this is possible; because you believed that together we could become far more than the sum of our parts, and we did. We became greater, and we continue to grow by leaps and bounds every year, lighting fires in every environment we touch, because once others see what we have, they want to be a part of it—they want this trust, this strength, this unstoppable power that we've built together.

"What we've done together is phenomenal! And it's humbling. I know that each of you will continue to carry on the spirit that we actively, passionately generate here in the Phossium family, and that you will have the moral courage to stand for it regardless of circumstance . . .

. . . because you are capable of it, and I will always believe in you."

She stopped to brush the tears from her cheeks one more time, then concluded, "Thank you, all of you, for showing me what's truly possible when people are able to come together in trust, as one mind, and in complete alignment on the job at hand. Together, you will illuminate the world."

With that, she held up her glass. "Cheers!" she said, and everyone in the room joined her, glasses raised, cheered, and then applauded so hard that the walls seemed to vibrate.

Carolyn looked over at Hugh with a smile of both unfathomable joy and sorrow. She took her hand away from her chest where she'd been holding it and gently pressed the delicate paper into his hands. "Here," she said. "You might need this some day." She hugged him one last time and added, "And I know you're going to do an incredible job as CEO. Phossium is in the best of hands."

STRIKE A MATCH

A FIELD GUIDE FOR SPARKING A PEAK PERFORMANCE CULTURE

DISCIPLINE IS

REMEMBERING

WHAT YOU

WANT.

LAO TSU

I f you jumped right to Part II from the introduction, you're aware that this is the Field Guide—your how-to manual for implementing a peak performance culture in your organization. If you've read Carolyn's story as well, then this is your opportunity to take a straightforward look at the disciplines that she and her team implemented as they developed their own peak performance culture. For the sake of clarity, we'll call these the *ways of being* and *disciplines to practice* for supporting a peak performance culture.

Creating and sustaining a peak performance culture requires a disciplined approach over time. For example, you can go to the store and buy a quality bowling ball, but that doesn't make you a great bowler. Being a good bowler is generated and sustained through regular and disciplined practice, just as love and health and physical fitness all need to be generated each and every day in order to sustain them. The same goes for a peak performance culture.

What follows is a three-part action plan for sparking a peak performance culture:

Section #1: Six Steps to Strike That First Match – This will explain how you can jumpstart the peak performance culture process, enroll some friends, and see immediate results.

Section #2: What Is Culture? – Here you will get grounded on what culture is and become clear on how to explain culture to others, helping them see the importance of being intentional when it comes to shaping it.

Section #3: The 3 Ways of Being and the 7 Disciplines of a Peak Performance Culture – The final section will outfit you with what you need to spark a peak performance culture, showing you how to eliminate the behaviors that do not support it.

SIX STEPS TO STRIKE THE FIRST MATCH

This will explain how you can jump start the process, enroll some friends, and see immediate results.

STEP 1

The next few pages explain what culture is and why it is important. Once you understand this, help your associates get the same clarity. There is no sense in going forward if you can't get folks to care. Take a pass at making your current culture clear; think about the consequences and implications of your current culture persisting and ask yourself, "Does culture eat strategy for lunch?"—as thought leader Edward Deming claimed in the 1980s.

STEP 2

What follows is a comprehensive view of a peak performance culture. Get some folks together and talk about these lists. Do they make sense to everyone? What's missing? What's confusing? What sounds interesting? Get folks talking.

THE ONLY SOURCE OF KNOWLEDGE IS EXPERIENCE.

—ALBERT EINSTEIN

STEP 3

Enroll some of your organization's leadership to join in. Make it easy for them. Or, if you are the top person, bring in some of your most promising staff to join you. Leave the "Debbie Downers" out for now, as the energy they waste is too much to deal with in the early stages of culture work.

STEP 4

Agree to go deeper in bite sizes. Take on each of the *three foundational ways of being* (See page 331) one at a time. Carve out some meeting time for each one. I have included some focusing questions that should help get things moving. At the end of each bite-size meeting, ask yourselves, "So what? Did what we talked about really matter? Should we act on what we now know?" Remind people of the Chinese proverb that says, "To know and not to act is not to know."

STEP 5

Make a request of your group to commit to living some or all aspects of a peak performance culture, reminding them that the commitment must be made with integrity. Start wherever the group feels like starting. Be kind. You are offering people an opportunity to transform behavior at a very personal level. Focus less on fixing problems and more on what might be possible.

STEP 6

Make a habit of revisiting the ways of being and disciplines to practice of a peak performance culture routinely, and make sure everybody is motivated and comfortable with calling out any breaches. Make sure new employees are aware of this.

In following these steps, I believe you will be wildly successful in striking your match and illuminating your organization's peak performance culture. Most people will be drawn into the light. They are waiting for you. However, as your peak performance culture gains power, it will reveal a certain group of people who will never engage with it. Their fierce resistance is less about the stand you are taking and more about who they choose to be. On pages 391-392, I will outline who they are, what motivates them, and how you can deal with them.

Here we go.

GIVE UP "SOMETHING IS WRONG."

CHOOSE WHAT IS.

WHAT IS CULTURE

Wisdom is the correct naming of things

CONFUCIUS

————

ulture is the line that every group draws that separates the behaviors they will tolerate and even advocate for from the behaviors that they will not tolerate.

**BEHAVIORS WE TOLERATE
AND ADVOCATE**

———————————————

**BEHAVIORS WE
DO NOT TOLERATE**

CULTURE

The key word here is "tolerate." Just because a behavior is above or below your group's culture line does not make it "good" or "bad." Do people use curse words in your office? If so, that behavior is above the line. Are people called out if they come late to meetings? If so, 'being late' goes below the line. Are goals and objectives missed without consequences? If so, 'missing goals' goes above the line. Look around you. The behaviors you observe and experience are the ones that are above the line, and those that result in immediate complaints from peers belong below the line.

The Line – There is *always* a line. You may not see it, but you always feel it. And where that line is drawn has huge implications on people's experience at work, recruiting, organizational performance, and your organization's ability to evolve over time.

New Eyes – When new people join your organization, they immediately start to figure out where this culture line is drawn. They automatically begin to catalogue the behaviors they see around them and are especially curious about the behaviors that are not tolerated. In a very real sense, this is a matter of survival.

"New eyes see what old eyes miss."

"A fish doesn't know there's water."

Take a moment to put some new eyes on, soften your gaze, walk the halls of your business, and "see" the existing culture. Reach out to a new employee and ask what they are seeing. Does their assessment of your organization's culture look like your own? What are they seeing that you might be missing?

Drawing The Line – The culture line gets drawn in one of three ways. Which one best describes your circumstance?

DEFAULT

These are the organizations that let the chips fall where they may. They are living in a culture that happens on its own with no stated intention about what the culture should be and no disciplined approach to shaping it.

STATED & INCONGRUENT

These are the organizations that take the time to talk about and make posters about the culture they want to have. Here you see a collection of aspirational and pithy phrases like "collaborative," "open," "honest," "customer driven," "caring," "fun," "supportive," "loyal," and other such niceties. But there is no disciplined approach to living these aspirations, and the behaviors that people experience on a daily basis often run counter to these ideals. An incongruence exists between the stated culture and the experienced culture. This is extremely common. In these circumstances, there is typically no effort to document the culture that actually exists.

INTENTIONAL AND CONGRUENT

These are the organizations that write down the behaviors they will tolerate and advocate for, as well as the ones they will not tolerate. They also take the next step to empower all employees to call out any employee immediately upon recognition that they are acting in a manner that is not congruent with the stated culture. These organizations lean in relentlessly to ensure that what is experienced is congruent with what is stated. These organizations know that culture is too important to be left to chance. They also refuse to allow breaches of integrity by saying one thing but doing another.

HOW DOES CULTURE FIT IN WITH RULES, LAWS, AND POLICIES?

Culture is one of THREE drivers of behavior. Understanding the other two will help you better understand culture:

YOU MUST
RULES AND POLICIES

WE OUGHT
CULTURE

I OUGHT
PERSONAL MORAL COMPASS

OUGHT

Personal Moral Compass – This is that little voice in our heads that says "I ought do this" and "I ought *not* to do that." People tend to follow their personal moral compass even when no one is looking. For instance, some people would not even take a paperclip from the company's supply room for personal use, while others use it as their kid's personal school-supply resource. Screening for people with appropriate personal moral compasses is the most cost effective and powerful ways to shape organizational performance.

Culture – This is the little voice in your group's collective head that says, "We ought to do this," and "We ought not do that." A toxic culture can overwhelm a personal moral compass at times. This is painful for the individual and a lost opportunity for the organization.

"A bad system will beat a good person every time."—W. Edwards Deming

Rules, Laws, and Policies – When people's personal moral compasses and the culture are no longer strong enough, these are a last-ditch effort to shape behavior. Rules, laws, and policies are the least effective and most expensive ways to shape behavior. This is because your personal moral compass and being a part of the culture around you are natural intrinsic values, while rules, laws, and policies are extrinsic; they are the booming voice of Big Brother saying *"You must."* Organizations that excessively rely on rules, laws, and policies become overly litigious, causing people to become compliant but not committed. Organizations that screen well for people with sound personal moral compasses and invest in generating peak performance cultures will naturally have a better work environment than a litigious organization every time.

WHY IS CULTURE SO IMPORTANT?

In the 1980s, management guru Edgar Schein wrote that "Culture determines the limit of strategy, and if you do not manage culture, it will manage you." Back then, other management and leadership gurus were saying things like "Culture eats strategy for breakfast."

Reflecting on his time as CEO of IBM in the 1990s, Lou Gerstner said that in his first three months on the job, he did not think one hour about culture. However, he later goes on to say that leading IBM taught him that "culture is everything—culture is king."

"CULTURE IS KING, AND CULTURE EATS ANYTHING IT WANTS ANYTIME IT WANTS."

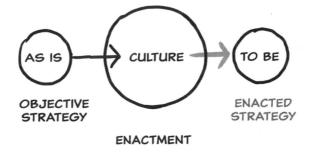

OBJECTIVE STRATEGY

ENACTMENT

ENACTED STRATEGY

Never in the thirty-plus years that I have been helping to drive organizational performance have I seen so much "C-level" interest in organizational culture. Across all sectors, leaders are telling me that they no longer buy into the myth of "technology determinism": 86 percent of investments into things like customer relationship management (CRM) and enterprise resource planning (ERP) fail to produce intended return on investment (ROI); e-organizations fail to deliver on intended results; and returns are not seen on investing in packaged methodologies like total quality management (TQM), Excellence

Plus, Agile, Spiral, Integrated DEFinition Methods (IDEF), Lean, business process reengineering (BPR), Six Sigma, and so on.

At a time when organizations need to establish and live by clear, strategic intentions, leaders continue to share with me their frustrations with the difficulty in turning their thoughts into real-world outcomes.

Leaders everywhere now know that the benefits of all these frameworks, technologies, and methods are only realized when they are applied within the context of a peak performance culture. Culture is what determines if and how our thoughts, ideas, and plans are enacted. Regardless of what you want to happen, culture determines what will happen.

This realization has created a thirst for practical ways to move from a default organizational culture—the one you have if you are not intentional about generating culture—to a peak performance culture that will operationalize your greatest intentions and create a great work-life experience.

The good news is that it is entirely possible to design and live a peak performance culture. We have done it in manufacturing and services companies from Silicon Valley to the US heartland, from big investment banks in lower Manhattan to emerging companies in Afghanistan, and in both the public and private sectors.

Now that we are clear on what culture is and why it is so important, we can delve into gaining a better understanding of peak performance culture and explore how you can spark one where you work, or wherever you find yourself involved in groups.

THE ESSENCE OF A PEAK PERFORMANCE CULTURE

3 Ways of Being

These are the table stakes. You and those around you either are or are not being this way, with the goal of always doing what you say, being clear about what you intend, and being persistent until outcomes are achieved.

Being Integrity

Honoring your word as your life.

Being Intentional

Getting what you want because you are clear about what you want.

Being Persistent

Enduring and adjusting actions until the outcome is achieved.

7 Disciplines to Practice

These are what you always hold as important and relentlessly seek to master.

Interconnectedness / Interdependency

Making "over there" disappear

Power

Alignment of key people regarding critical things

Possibility

Giving up "something is wrong"

Moral Courage

Standing on principle, in danger, for as long as it takes

Social Contracting

Assignment of actions

Customer

Keeping the main thing the main thing

Feedback

Conversing for learning and growth

READING ABOUT

MAKING A CAKE

IS NOTHING LIKE

MAKING A CAKE.

BE YOUR WORD

Let your yes be yes and your no be no.

JESUS, AS RECORDED BY MATTHEW IN 36 AD

———

I n a peak performance culture, when people say "yes" they mean "yes." When people give their word, regardless of whether it relates to a big or small thing, everybody knows that it is as good as done. No one drops the ball. Meetings start on time. Reports are finalized and delivered when promised. Workability is high. As a result, people and the organization itself are considered trustworthy.

WHAT IS INTEGRITY?

Integrity is the acceptance that your word and your life are interchangeable and that you unfailingly come through on your promises. This does not make your *actions* right or wrong. Living in integrity is not moral. You could say you were going to do a bad thing and then do it, and be living in integrity. You could also say you were going to do a good thing and then do it, and still be living in integrity.

INTEGRITY

Breaches of integrity abound in our daily lives. We sit around, waiting past our appointment time to see our doctor. Products fail to live up to advertisements. Coworkers cannot be relied on to follow through on commitments. Politicians say one thing to get elected but do something else when in office. We tell our children "I'll be there in a second." So why is honoring your word as your life important?

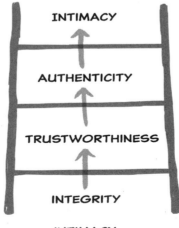

Because being your word in all matters makes you trustworthy, and people will learn to trust you. When those around you trust you, they are inclined to be authentic in sharing with you, and this authenticity leads to wholeness.

Think, for instance, about your car.

When you start your car, that ignition switch links to wires that link to a starter system that link to the engine. Dozens of parts must do exactly what they're designed to do—what they "say" they're going to do—so that your car will start.

In and of themselves, each part is whole and does what it's designed to do. When the parts are working together, each one is expected to know what to do when the previous part signals to it. Each part expects the signal to come exactly as it's supposed to, and when it does, that part is expected to act exactly as it's supposed to, and the next part is expected to do the same.

In doing what it's designed to do, your car has integrity.

Companies and organizations are the same.

In a way, the people in a company are parts. Each person relies on the other to do his or her job in a dependable way; that the output will be there when it's supposed to be, in the manner promised, so that it serves as input for the next person to complete his or her task. And so on.

The integrity of the whole is the integrity of each part, and the integrity of each part is only as good as the part it touches. Each part must hold its integrity, doing as it's supposed to do in the way it's supposed to do it so that it interacts in a predictable way and the whole system becomes trustworthy.

A peak performance culture is not possible until this relationship exists, and it is not easy to establish. It takes effort. Just as a person doesn't become a world-class weight lifter after one day at the gym, a peak performance culture does not exist unless it's actively maintained.

Integrity is the skeletal system of your culture. It is the ironworks, the operating system, the engine of peak performance.

Integrity, the source of trustworthiness, is as vital as air. Build this and you've built the foundation for limitless possibilities.

Years ago, there was an entrepreneur named Donald Burr who started a discount airline called PEOPLExpress. Don was passionate about the importance of people keeping their word and often used a very clear example when speaking about it at forums and industry events.

When people arrived at the airport for one of his flights, he explained, the process was pretty simple. They purchased a low-fare ticket, moved down to the gate, and got on the plane, all in a clean and efficient manner.

They would then get in the seat, strap in, and the plane would take off right on time. Everything's fine. They're rocking and rolling and satisfied with the whole process. Then the plane reaches cruising altitude and they see a meal cart coming down the aisle, so they pull down a plastic tray table—and there in the upper right-hand corner is a tiny squished green bean from the flight before.

In that moment, Don explained, that passenger becomes absolutely certain that the mechanics on the airplane left a wrench in the engine or didn't tighten a propeller as well as they should have. They become convinced that everyone on that plane is going to die.

It's not because of the green bean. It's because the airline failed to do something.

Of all the people he paid, Don would say, the people he paid the least were those who cleaned the plane between shifts, and yet because of a failure on that part of the operation, he just took a huge hit on a brand that took him $100 million to create.

"There are no big and small promises: There is only your word," Don concluded. "Your life is on the line when you give your word, every single time."

A peak performance culture is not given; it's not something you can just "have." It is actively, constantly generated. People's belief in your integrity doesn't happen overnight—you must persist in it. It has to become foundational to who you are in order for it to generate a sense of trustworthiness.

At the same time, however, we are all humans. Breaches will happen. Unforeseen circumstances occur. But what you *shouldn't* do when you fail to keep a promise is ignore it. Breaches *have* to be acknowledged.

If you said you were going to do something and didn't, acknowledge it. And in the future, you will. Clean up the breach without upset and move on.

On the flip side of that, in standing for integrity and striving for it in our culture, we must expect the same out of others. We must expect their best, and they should hear that from us. When we start to talk about other people's failings behind their backs, we create gossip, and gossip does nothing but harm. At the same time, however, we don't want people to feel as though they're wrong for lacking integrity. Instead, we want them to know that we believe in them, in their integrity, and in their trustworthiness, and that we are intolerant of anything less than their full power.

SHAPE YOUR CULTURE

ANSWER THE FOLLOWING QUESTIONS ON YOUR OWN:

Keeping in mind that giving your word means giving your word, and that there are no big or small promises, how would those who know you best assess your integrity?

How would you rate the integrity of those around you?

How would your life change if you took on honoring your word as your life in all matters?

ANSWER THE FOLLOWING QUESTIONS AS A GROUP:

Collectively, what do we as an organization tolerate and not tolerate with respect to integrity?

What are the consequences and implications of this way of being?

How would our lives change if we all agreed to live in integrity with those around us?

INTENTION UNLOCKS ALL THE **GIFTS OF THE UNIVERSE.**

BE INTENTIONAL

YOUR CHANCES OF GETTING WHAT YOU WANT GO UP AS YOU BECOME CLEARER ABOUT WHAT YOU WANT.

"What are you up to?"

The response to this question tells you whether the person you ask is intentional or not. Some folks will have a clear answer. They will respond with some variation of:

> **"I am going. . ."**

> **"I am doing. . ."**

> **"I am going to be. . ."**

Others will furrow their eyebrows and try to engage you in their quest to answer the question, because in the moment they simply do not know.

Intentionality is critical, because it allows you to access all the help around you. Intentional people and intentional organizations get assistance from the universe. Unintentional people get compassion, at best, and unintentional organizations eventually get squished by their environment.

Consider these two scenarios.

A director of marketing and sales for a mid-sized systems integrator is at a party and is asked, "So, what are you trying to do with your company these days?"

The director could say, "Well, we're trying to figure that out. We know we want to grow; we're just trying to figure out how and where." To which the person who asked the question may say something like, "I see. Well, I am going to refresh my drink."

But what if the director had said, "We are going to establish a foothold in the systems deployment organization of the US Air Force (USAF). I am looking for a contact in the Pentagon acquisition office."

To which the person who asked the question may reply, "That's interesting. My wife's sister works in the USAF Chief Information Officer (CIO) Office in the Pentagon. She might be able to help you sort out who is who in acquisition. Would you like to talk to her?"

The clear intention in the latter scenario creates the possibility for help to arrive. In a peak performance culture, the people and the organization, as a whole, maintain a posture of clear, shared intention, enabling the universe to assist in surprising ways.

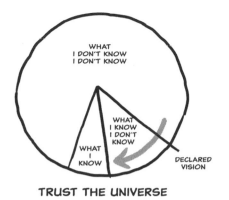

TRUST THE UNIVERSE

Every now and then, people and organizations need to go into their "planning closets" to privately try to figure out or refine their intention. Peak performance culture, however, believes this:

1) One should always occur as intentional in public. Never be unintentional in public.

2) It is okay to reassess your intention privately, quickly, and not too often.

3) You win the game by acting from shared intention on the court. Reassessing your intention in the locker room is at times necessary and is always hard.

4) There is no risk in planning, but there is also no winning in planning. The risk of failure is in acting, and acting is the only way to win.

5) Powerful action is the result of deeply shared intention. Fragmented or unclear intention limits performance.

SHAPE YOUR CULTURE

ANSWER THE FOLLOWING QUESTIONS ON YOUR OWN:

What kind of person do you intend to be?

What kind of life do you intend to live?

What are you making happen regarding your job?

*What is your intention regarding causing a
peak performance culture at work?*

ANSWER THE FOLLOWING QUESTIONS AS A GROUP:

What kind of company do we intend to create?

What kind of experience do we all want to share at work?

BE PERSISTENT

ENDURING AND ADJUSTING ACTIONS
UNTIL OUTCOME IS ACHIEVED

Persistence is observable and is a foundational *way of being* for those who intend to cause and live in a peak performance culture. Persistence in this context is relentlessly acting to achieve an intended outcome and adjusting those actions when blocked or when smarter actions become apparent to achieve those intended outcomes.

We all know the people who, when given an assignment, stop making progress on the assignment the minute they run into an unexpected block. These are the folks who come back to you saying "I can't find this" or "Can you help me with that" or "Here is something we did not consider, and I do not know what to do."

On the other hand, there are the Rowans of the world. In 1898, war broke out between Spain and the United States, and Cuba was in the center of it all. President McKinley needed to get a letter to General Garcia, the leader of the insurgents, who was somewhere in the uncharted interior mountains of the island-nation, and someone suggested the young Lieutenant Andrew Summers Rowan.

The story goes that Rowan was sent for, given the letter, and shortly thereafter he disappeared into the jungles of Cuba under the cover of night. Three weeks later, Rowan came out the other side of the island having completed his mission.

That is what he did. But more important was what he did *not* do. He did not ask "Who is Garcia?" "How do I find him?" "Why is this important?" or "Who is going to help me?" Instead, Lieutenant Rowan persisted.

This story is beautifully captured in Elbert Hubbard's novelette *A Message To Garcia*, published in 1899 and distributed more widely than any book of its time. Regarding Rowan, Elbert writes:

PERSIST

> "By the eternal! There is a man whose form should be cast in deathless bronze and the statue placed in every college of the land. It is not book-learning young men need, nor instruction about this, and that, but a stiffing of the vertebrae which will cause them to be loyal to a trust, to act promptly, concentrate their energies: do the thing—Carry the message to Garcia!"

Intentions are mere aspirations in the absence of persistence. Honoring your word as your life and living in integrity will require your persistence, and a universe that enjoys surprises will require your persistence to drive various actions.

SHAPE YOUR **CULTURE**

ANSWER THE FOLLOWING QUESTIONS ON YOUR OWN:

When have you been Rowan? What did that feel like?

When have you let blocks thwart your progress?

How do you think you occur to others regarding grit and persistence?

ANSWER THE FOLLOWING QUESTIONS AS A GROUP:

To what degree do you value and reward persistence?

Who among your organization is most Rowan-esque?

What would it be like for everybody to be like Rowan?

TO KNOW AND NOT TO ACT

IS NOT

TO KNOW.

———

LAO TSU

SEVEN DISCIPLINES

(DISCIPLINES TO CONTINUOUSLY MASTER)

CUSTOMER

Keeping the main thing the main thing

FEEDBACK

Conversing for learning and growth

INTERCONNECTEDNESS / INTERDEPENDENCY

Making "over there" disappear

POSSIBILITY

Giving up "something is wrong"

SOCIAL CONTRACTING

Assignment of actions

POWER

Alignment of key people regarding critical things

MORAL COURAGE

Standing on principle, in danger, for as long as it takes

The table stakes are down. You and your team are living in integrity with each other and your customers, you're clear on your intentions, and you have agreed to be persistent until your intentions are realized. These agreements alone will radically enhance your organizational performance. Yet you keep reading this guide because you are seeking peak performance. Your intentions are:

1) **To place the soul of your organization in the unmet needs of the marketplace and make your customers' voice the dominant signal throughout your company.** You want to make it so that everyone hears and prioritizes the unmet needs of your customers and prospects.

2) **To eliminate the destructive force of gossip and to live in a place where feedback is seen as an expression of caring**—where your peers, customers, and suppliers thirst to receive that feedback and have mastery in providing it.

3) **To make clear how your peers, customers, and suppliers are interconnected and interdependent,** and to support the people around you in their relentless efforts to figure out better ways to act to have an enhanced effect on others.

4) **To make "what is possible?" the reflexive response to any unforeseen developments** instead of the energy-draining thought of "something is wrong."

5) **To be effective and efficient at requesting and commanding others to do things** and create an

environment where all can be comfortable saying "no" to requests when it is the appropriate response.

6) **To be able to generate sufficient power to achieve any intention** because your key people are deeply aligned.

7) **To reward those who take a stand for principles they deem critical**, regardless of how dangerous it is for them to take that stand, and to make this the reflexive response to all developments.

We begin with the main discipline to practice—the customer.

PEOPLE HAVE NOT CHANGED MUCH SINCE CREATION.

AND THEY NEVER WILL.

THE CUSTOMER

Being intentional, being persistent, and honoring your word as your life are what it takes to play. But what game are you playing? The people in a peak performance culture are clear and aligned on the game that they are playing. That is, they exist primarily for meeting the unmet needs of the marketplace in a manner that enables the company to grow profitably.

The people of a peak performance culture:

1) Have a shared understanding of who their prospects and customers are

2) Are aligned on what their customers and prospects are trying to do and what they think is making that effort difficult for them to accomplish

3) Understand the consequences of not meeting the unmet needs of their customers and prospects

4) Have a clear sense of what they contribute to customers and prospects when they fully meet their unmet needs in a cost-effective manner

5) Are relentless in making their company the perfect conduit for interfacing with, and providing value to, all aspects of customer interaction

6) Fix first anything that negatively affects the customers' realization of value

7) First and always make excellent what customers touch and experience

8) Do whatever they must to be certain that they understand what the market needs and how their company is occurring to their current customers

9) Unleash the customers' voices inside the consciousness of all its employees

As of this writing, so much of leadership's time is being consumed with how to manage Millennials and how to build workspace for the new employees entering the workforce. We obsess about 360-degree feedback, opinion surveys, career counseling, mentoring, and other inwardly focused "flavors of the day."

All this inward focus may have a place in a busy day, but it should never be at the expense of the customer—the number-one source of power in any organization.

SOURCES OF POWER

Any business leader will benefit from understanding where the sources of power are for their organizations and orienting themselves to what matters most. The following image represents this orientation in the form of a compass:

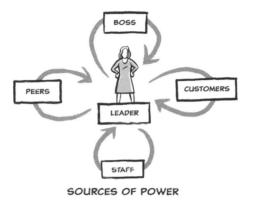

SOURCES OF POWER

To her north are her bosses, board of directors, and shareholders.

To her south are her employees.

To her west are her peers and competitors.

To her east are her markets and her current customers.

The leader must generate and sustain sufficient power to lead her company forward and be crystal clear on the best way to generate her power. For instance:

Spending time in the south generates very little power—If a leader focuses primarily on spending time with her staff to understand their needs and desires and to help them conduct their business, she generates very little power with either her bosses or her customers. Her bosses will see her efforts as simply a part of her job, and the customers will have no visibility into her actions and may not care as much as she does about the needs of her staff. Additionally, she generates little power with her peers and competitors.

Spending time in the west generates some north and south power, but not much—Attending industry conferences and joining affinity groups offer great personal value and can generate some credibility and power for a leader in the north and south, as it would make her seem more rounded and aware of market dynamics, but it doesn't offer a lot of power. Customers often have little interest in what conferences you attend and what groups you belong to.

Spending time in the north generates some south and west power—When a leader spends time cultivating deep relationships with her bosses, those efforts are noticed by her staff in the south. They like having their boss liked by her boss, and the west often notices that she has endeared herself with upper management. However, it's easy to overplay this and create accidental adversaries, and, ultimately, customers really do not care.

Spending time in the east generates enormous power in the north, south, and west—The leader must finally understand that she is most powerful in the north, south, and west when she understands the east better than anyone. Continually making meaningful and direct communication with her customers her number-one priority will enable her to *take on their voice with credibility* as she moves through the south, west, and north.

It's important to note, however, that the leader should not discount the importance of spending time with her staff, bosses, peers, and competitors. Instead, she should just know that she is most effective, most powerful, and in the best position to help in these realms when she speaks with the indisputable authority of the customers' voice.

In a peak performance culture, the conversation begins and ends with the customer:

1) Everyone knows that the soul of their company lies in the unmet needs of the marketplace, and this soul calls on the strength of the company to meet these needs. People of a peak performance company get that their company exists to produce external value, first and foremost.

2) Everyone in the organization knows what is meant by the word *customer*. A customer is always *external*. He or she is the person who authorizes the conveyance of cash in order to secure the company's products or services. Keep in mind that Mattel Toy Company gets its cash from selling toys to Toys "R" Us and other retailers and wholesalers. They are its customers. Parents are the customers of Toys "R" Us because they pay for the toys for their children. Children are consumers of the Mattel products. They are not the customers.

3) Everyone can link what he or she does to the direct experience of the customer or a prospect that the company intends to become a customer. If he or she cannot see this link, then the employee should abandon the task, as it's likely a non-value added activity.

4) Everyone is intensely curious about, and is actively engaged in, listening to the *sounds of the east*. This sound—which includes the voice of the customers, their unmet needs, their strategic direction, how they measure their success and the things that are making it hard for them, and how they see your company—is amplified and unleashed in the physical and cyber hallways of every organization.

5) Everyone is continuously and relentlessly searching for the best way to fully understand the customer in a manner that produces the most insight in a way that is least intrusive on the customer's time.

6) Finally, everyone understands that raises, promotions, career paths, training budgets, fringe benefits, incentives and bonuses, and investments in workspace and tools are all a derivative of *customer value creation*.

SHAPE YOUR **CULTURE**

ANSWER THE FOLLOWING QUESTIONS ON YOUR OWN:

*How do your daily tasks directly contribute
to building value for customers?*

*How do you know what your customers think
about the value they receive from you?*

*How much of your time do you spend thinking about
your customers versus any other topics?*

ANSWER THE FOLLOWING QUESTIONS AS A GROUP:

Talk as a group until you are deeply aligned on the answers to
the following:

Who, specifically, are our customers?

What are they trying to accomplish?

What is making that hard for them?

How do our products and services contribute to their success?

How can we increase the value we are providing?

TRUTH IS DESCRIBING THINGS AS THEY REALLY ARE.

FEEDBACK

CONVERSING FOR LEARNING AND GROWTH

In a peak performance culture, giving feedback is seen as an outward expression of caring. Similarly, people's reception of and action on feedback is seen as an outward expression of commitment to mastery, both personal and organizational.

Essentially, feedback is a gift offered freely from one person to another with the sole purpose being to benefit the receiver. Nothing is expected in return. This is an important point, because mastery of feedback requires distinguishing feedback from problem solving.

SCENARIO

Consider Bob. He is routinely late for team meetings and is often unprepared, so Claire, the team leader, decides to intervene:

Scenario #1: Claire approaches Bob and says, "Bob, your tardiness and lack of sufficient preparation are having a detrimental effect on the team's overall performance. You need to be on time and do what you say you are going to do so that the team can be capable of completing what it needs to do on time."

Scenario #2: Claire approaches Bob and says, "Bob, I need to share something with you, and my motive is for you to be a relevant and powerful part of our team. You know integrity is a shared value in our group, and lately, you have not been occurring to the rest of us as a person of integrity. You have been late. And you have been unprepared. I refuse to tolerate anything other than you being your best self. Endless possibilities are in front of you if we feel we can trust and depend on you. That happens when you are seen as trustworthy, and trustworthiness is a function of honoring your word as your life. Do you understand that I am sharing this with you because I genuinely care for you?"

Scenario #3: Claire approaches a coworker, Mary, and says, "Do you see how Bob is always late? We are always waiting for him, and he is so undependable. He's really putting all of us at risk. I am so upset with him."

EXPLANATION

Scenario #1 is *problem-solving*. As team leader, Claire's motive is to make a problem she is experiencing go away. She is the only one getting the benefit of the conversation.

Scenario #2 is *feedback*. Claire's motive is to take a stand for Bob and his future. She is speaking with Bob strictly for his benefit, because she cares.

Scenario #3 is *gossip*. This is the most destructive force in any organization—more on that in a minute.

You can discern feedback from problem-solving by examining the motive: Is the communication being done for the benefit of the speaker or the person receiving it? Feedback is essential in a peak performance culture and can result in:

1) Team members understanding how to continuously, effectively, and efficiently solicit rich feedback from customers, prospects, colleagues, and shareholders.

2) Each person committing to offer generative, timely feedback to each other—continuously, effectively, and efficiently.

3) Each person committing to making it easy for others to give him or her feedback and acting on that feedback him- or herself.

To make this vital communication happen, however, the people in a peak performance culture must master the art of giving and receiving feedback, and mastery requires more than just the right message. In fact, it requires five different "rights:"

✓ **RIGHT MESSAGE**

✓ **RIGHT TIME**

✓ **RIGHT PERSON**

✓ **RIGHT WAY**

✓ **RIGHT REASON**

FEEDBACK AS CARING

First, you must craft the *right message*. There is a big difference between telling people they are "always late" versus telling them that they are losing their place in the group because they are "breaching their word" and are "seen as undependable." When planning to offer feedback, take the time to craft a message that speaks to the heart of what is going on from the perspective of the people who are receiving the feedback. They already know that they're often late. What they might not know is that this behavior is affecting their standing in the group and their possibilities for the future.

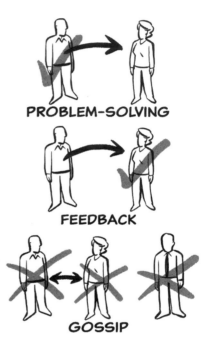

PROBLEM-SOLVING

FEEDBACK

GOSSIP

Mastery of feedback also means determining the right time to offer that feedback: a time that is determined by the person receiving the feedback, not the person offering it. For instance, if she were a master of feedback, Claire would have said to Bob, "I've got some feedback for you. When would be a good time for you and me to talk?" Offering the receiver this degree of control reduces anxiety and facilitates the capacity to listen.

Additionally, feedback needs to be offered to the right person. This may seem obvious, but it is a step that is widely violated, and that violation has a very special name: gossip. In the context of a peak performance culture, gossip is when two or more people talk about a third person in a manner that leaves the third person diminished in the eyes of the group with no one committed to sharing that feedback with the third person. Gossip is the most destructive force in any organization. The person gossiping is destroying the standing of a fellow employee while not building any value for customers. The person listening is also enabling that destruction while not building any customer value. Neither are offering the third person a chance to learn and grow.

A peak performance culture is intolerant of *gossip*. The most effective way to eliminate gossip from your organization is not to listen to it. In a peak performance culture, when one person begins sharing derogatory stories about another, the listener quickly interrupts and asks:

> **"Why are you telling me this? Is it:**
>
> 1) **So I can help you offer feedback to this person?**
>
> 2) **Because you want me to offer this feedback to this person?**
>
> **If neither, then there's no reason for you to tell me this."**

By not tolerating gossip, a peak performance culture does not give it a place to fester—and it dies.

Mastery of feedback also means giving feedback in the *right* way, and the right way is not determined by the preferences of the person *offering* the feedback. Instead, the right way is the way that the person receiving the feedback will hear it best.

For instance, some people require being hit with a four by four just to get their attention. Others need only the slightest brush of a feather to hear the message loud and clear. This burden is on the person *offering* the feedback. It's up to him or her to convey it in the manner most suited to the person receiving it.

Finally, mastery of feedback means giving feedback for the *right* reason, and there is only one right reason: when the person *giving* it has a true sense of caring for the recipient.

Mastery of feedback does not make it easy to give or receive. In fact, it's often an awkward and uncomfortable conversation for both parties. But the people in a peak performance culture do it because they are committed to a relentless pursuit of organizational and personal growth, and they know that the source of this growth is feedback.

FEEDBACK FROM CUSTOMERS: FIRST, SECOND, AND THIRD ORDER QUESTIONS

When it comes to getting feedback from customers, a peak performance culture not only values customer feedback above all else, but it has also mastered the art of effectively soliciting that feedback.

Assuming the right time, place, person, message, and reason, the people of a peak performance culture know how to go deep with customers. This begins by thanking customers for their time, and committing, with integrity, to act on everything that customer shares.

They then ask **first order** questions, like:

- How are things going?
- Are you getting what you need?
- Is there anything we can be doing differently?

To these rather tame questions, the customers typically give tame answers. But the people of a peak performance culture are just warming up!

Next, they move on to **second order** questions, like:

- What are you trying to do with your business and what is making that hard for you?
- Tell me about anything that we are providing you, and how we are providing it, that is at all less than perfect.
- If you were me, what would you want to know about you? What do you wish I asked about our relationship?

Customers typically respond with more feedback that is deeper and more nuanced.

Finally, the people of a peak performance culture move on to **third order** questions, such as:

- What motivates you to refer us to one of your most trusted peers?
- What would cause you to hesitate in any way to refer us to one of your most valued and trusted peers?
- What would an absolutely ideal relationship between our organizations look like?

The people of a peak performance culture are adamant about understanding their customers' responses to first, second, and third order questions, because those replies are all seen as possibilities. They're treated like gold, and each response is acted on with integrity, intentionality, and persistence.

SHAPE YOUR **CULTURE**

ANSWER THE FOLLOWING QUESTIONS ON YOUR OWN:

*How do you describe the timeliness and quality
of the feedback you are getting?*

*How do you describe the quality and timeliness
of the feedback you provide others?*

*What role do you currently play in tolerating or
not tolerating gossip in your organization?*

ANSWER THE FOLLOWING QUESTIONS AS A GROUP:

*How would you describe the value your
organization places on feedback?*

*How in depth, how useful, and how timely does
feedback flow throughout your organization?*

*How would you describe the quality and timeliness
of your customer-feedback process?*

*How certain are you that you have the full picture regarding
how your customers feel about your organization?*

To what extent does your organization tolerate gossip?

What importance do you place on becoming intolerant of gossip?

INTERCONNECTEDNESS/ INTERDEPENDENCY

MAKING "OVER THERE" DISAPPEAR

The people of a peak performance culture agree with Dr. Martin Luther King Jr. when he said, *"Whatever affects one directly, affects all indirectly."* Through explicit and tight social contracting (see Discipline Five), they are clear about the interdependencies between all individuals. Mist in one area creates fog in another. They are one system made up of a series of subsystems, each composed of a number of people and things all committed to doing what they say they're going to do when they say they're going to do it.

When this happens, something amazing occurs. These peak-performance-culture organizations access the highest level of performance.

Which of the following statements best describes how things are occurring to you now?

LEVELS OF INTERCONNECTEDNESS AND INTERDEPENDENCY

- **Level 0**—Unit and department leaders are busy doing what they are doing. Period.

- **Level 1**—Unit and department leaders are aware of and acting to meet the unmet needs of their own organization. Unit growth and performance is celebrated.

- **Level 2**—Unit and department leaders are aware of and acting to meet the unmet needs of their own organization and are available when requested to help other unit and department leaders meet their own unmet needs. Unit growth and performance and cross-organizational assistance is celebrated.

- **Level 3**—Unit and department leaders are aware of and acting to meet the unmet needs of their own organization and are clear on the interconnectedness and interdependencies of all parts of the organization. As such, they are proactively seeking to understand the unmet needs of the entire organization and hold those needs as their own, acting to meet all the unmet needs of the organization. Whole-system optimization is celebrated.

MODELING INTERCONNECTEDNESS AND INTERDEPENDENCY

This shared perspective is often generated with the use of a model that visualizes each part of an organization and how those parts are interconnected and interdependent.

A good model should answer the following questions for everyone in the organization:

1) What are all the parts?

2) How does each part contribute to the customer or shareholder experience?

3) What does each part depend on to do what it is supposed to do?

4) What are the consequences and implications of a breach of any part on the overall performance of the organization?

5) What current activities are not essential and should be eliminated?

6) Where should we be measuring to ensure rhythmic and peak performance?

7) What part of our system is currently constraining our growth and performance?

A good model is the rock star of new-employee orientation. Models are used as the basis for determining strategic intention, and models always include the customer. The model establishes shared perspective among all stakeholders in the organization.

Now for the very good news: The model you need for generating this shared perspective has probably already been drawn up. You see, there are really only about five business models:

- **Product:** makes and sells physical products (i.e., Black & Decker, Harley Davidson)
- **Service:** sells time (i.e. law firms, consultancies, system integrators)
- **Operation:** sells a capability
- **Channel:** organization connecting makers and buyers (i.e., Amazon)
- **Exchanges:** establishes and brokers the market between many buyers and many sellers

When this shared perspective exists, it also leads the people of a peak performance culture to share the following beliefs:

1) There is no "over there"—the actions of one person or one department in an organization impacts every other part of the business. There are no "silos."

2) All individuals in the organization can draw a clear line of sight from what they do to the creation of value for their customers and shareholders. If they can't establish this sight line with any given action, then they should eliminate the activity.

3) They understand that their organization is interacting with customers directly on all levels, from the way the phone is answered to the communications that customers receive, and they strive to make the customer's every experience world class.

4) They can see the direct connection between timely and accurate completion of back-office functions like timesheets and monthly status reports to the ability of the organization to manage cash and pay on time.

5) They know that if any part of the organization is suffering, then the entire organization Is affected and feeling the pain.

INTERCONNECTEDNESS / INTERDEPENDENCY

SHAPE YOUR **CULTURE**

ANSWER THE FOLLOWING QUESTIONS ON YOUR OWN:

How would you describe the link between what you do and the value delivered to a customer?

Who do you depend on to do your job?

Who depends on what you do to do their job?

ANSWER THE FOLLOWING QUESTIONS AS A GROUP:

How would customers be affected if you stopped doing all the things you do?

What are the top unmet needs of your organization, and how much time are you spending on meeting those unmet needs?

Which "Level of Interconnectedness and Interdependency" (0, 1, 2, or 3) best describes how your organization is currently operating? What are the tangible consequences and implications of this level of performance?

POSSIBILITY

GIVING UP "SOMETHING IS WRONG"

"What is possible now?"

This is the automatic response that people in a peak performance culture have to any circumstance. In fact, the overall context of a peak performance culture is "Possibility":

a) What is possible for our customers?
b) What is possible for our staff?
c) What is possible for our shareholders?
d) What is possible for the world because we exist in it?

Sure, organizations that are generating peak performance cultures face problems just like everyone else, but most of the time they give up coming from the direction of "something is wrong" and instead focus on "what is possible here?"

This difference is far more than just semantics—this is context, and context is decisive. Let's compare and contrast the context of "problem-solving" with the context of "possibility":

When action is called for from the context of "something is wrong and we need to fix it," we *only* see it as a problem that needs to be fixed. So we concentrate on doing the things that will fix the problem—and when we're done, we typically end up with what we had before, and not much more.

However, if we face an unexpected event from the context of "what is possible here?" then our actions are not limited to just solving the problem. Instead, we start to look beyond the problem and consider what is possible.

For example, say your car breaks down unexpectedly. That's a problem to solve, right? So, you concentrate on taking all the steps to get the car repaired and running again. You go to your mechanic and pressure him or her to fix the car as soon as possible because "it's a problem!"

From the perspective of possibility, however, if your car breaks down, what possibilities are created? If you've never tried ride-sharing, for instance, this would be the perfect opportunity to register with a company like Uber or Lyft and give them a try. So, instead of rushing to your mechanic and demanding that your car be fixed immediately, you say that you don't need it for a couple of weeks because you're using a rideshare, and it's actually saving you some time and money. The car breaking down has opened up a new possibility for you.

Possibility is an orientation. It is a context that stimulates innovation, growth, newness, and learning.

The people of a peak performance culture know that regardless of what confronts them, something is always possible. Possibility is one of the most enjoyable aspects of living with others in a peak performance culture.

SHAPE YOUR **CULTURE**

ANSWER THE FOLLOWING QUESTIONS ON YOUR OWN:

Why do you think the discipline of maintaining the "possibility reflex" has been identified as a discipline in a peak performance culture?

What problems are you currently solving, and what possibilities are you standing for?

How would giving up "something is wrong" and taking on "something is possible" affect your life and the lives of those you interact with?

ANSWER THE FOLLOWING QUESTIONS AS A GROUP:

To what degree is your organization's reputation one of problem-solving versus creating possibility?

How much value does your organization place on problem-solving versus the creation of possibility for customers, employees, and suppliers?

What are some real possibilities available to your organization right now?

What is the biggest possibility for customers that your organization can create?

What is the biggest possibility for employees that your organization can create?

WE SPEND
OUR LIVES
AVOIDING
THE SHAME
WE FELT AS
CHILDREN.

SOCIAL CONTRACTING

ASSIGNMENT OF ACTIONS

THE MASTERY OF CONVERSATIONS FOR ACTION

In a peak performance culture, language is used deliberately to cause action and get things done, so the stakes are high to master social contracting and conversing.

The people of a peak performance culture, for instance, take the time to understand two categories of distinctions related to social contracting and conversing. The first category focuses on conversing and distinguishes whether what is being said is a fact, a story, or a belief.

CONVERSING: FACTS, STORIES, AND BELIEFS

During most conversations, people fail to distinguish facts from stories from beliefs. It all sounds the same and is treated like it is the same. The people in a peak performance culture, however, are active listeners and understand the difference.

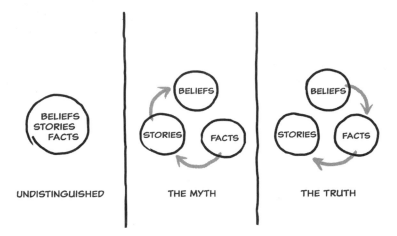

| UNDISTINGUISHED | THE MYTH | THE TRUTH |

FACTS, STORIES AND BELIEFS

Since language is important in a peak performance culture, what people say to one another is constantly challenged. Take the following examples of three typical statements:

- "We just got last month's sales numbers, and they look really bad. We look like a bunch of losers." (Story)

- "We just got last month's sales numbers, and they prove that our products are not relevant in today's market." (Belief)

- "We just got last month's sales numbers, and, collectively, we closed $22 million against our plan for that month against our $24 million target." (Fact)

The people working in a peak performance culture quickly realize that there are very few facts communicated when compared to how many beliefs and stories are shared every day.

- *Facts* are considered seriously.

- *Beliefs* are respected but challenged.

- *Stories* are considered to be personal interpretations and are usually seen as not binding or relevant.

SOCIAL CONTRACTING: STATEMENTS, REQUESTS, AND COMMANDS

The second distinction, social contracting, distinguishes statements from requests from commands:

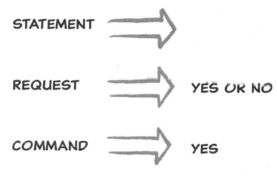

STATEMENT

REQUEST ⟹ YES OR NO

COMMAND ⟹ YES

REQUEST – COMMAND

- "That printer needs more paper." (Statement)

- "Frank, will you put more paper in the printer?" (Request)

- "Frank, put more paper in the printer." (Command)

This all seems straightforward enough, but in typical communication, commands and requests are often masquerading as statements. For instance, someone could make the statement, "It sure would be nice if someone put more paper in the printer," but an hour later, the printer would still be empty. He or she would be upset, but this upset would be unsubstantiated, because there was never a social contract established with someone else to take action.

Other times, commands masquerade as requests.

"Bernard, will you put paper in the printer?"

But if Bernard says he can't do that right now, the requester becomes upset. Although it was phrased as a request, responding "no" was not part of the option. Again, this format results in unsubstantiated upset.

In a peak performance culture, people are trained on clear social contracting to hear the difference between a statement, a request, and a command. No action is expected from a statement. Requests are made when the requester will accept a "yes" or "no" response without consequence.

Typically, someone makes a request. Then there is some negotiation that results in a "yes" or a "no" response. Because a peak performance culture has a bedrock of integrity, when someone says "yes" to a request, the action is as good as completed. Honoring your word as your life eliminates the need to check in or have status conversations to ensure things are getting done. In a peak performance culture, the person who is doing the task reports that it is "done," and the person making the request confirms that the task was done to their expectations. Once satisfied, the task is declared as "done–done."

Commands work pretty much the same way. A command is issued. Someone says "yes" and completes the task, and the requester then declares the action as "done-done." The only difference is that "no" is not an option.

Although commands are used sparingly, they can, in a peak performance culture, be issued by anyone to anyone. In peak performance cultures, people genuinely trust each other's motives. When a subordinate issues a command to a more senior person, the senior person assumes that the subordinate considered much, weighed tradeoffs, and concluded that it would be best for all concerned that the senior person be left with no response other than "yes."

In summary, in a peak performance culture, language is considered action. Facts, beliefs, and stories are distinguished and treated differently. Requests, statements, and commands are clearly distinguished and used appropriately, eliminating passive-aggressive interactions and confusion during social contracting.

SHAPE YOUR CULTURE

ANSWER THE FOLLOWING QUESTIONS ON YOUR OWN:

How easy or hard is it for you to ask others to do things?

*To what extent are you on the receiving end of
statements that are really requests or commands?*

*To what extent do you find yourself using passive language
and statements when asking others do things?*

ANSWER THE FOLLOWING QUESTIONS AS A GROUP:

*To what degree does your organization tolerate passive language
or requests and commands masquerading as statements?*

To what degree does your organization value the word "no?"

Across your organization, how easy is it to get others to do things?

POWER

ALIGNMENT OF KEY PEOPLE
REGARDING CRITICAL THINGS

hen an organization is at peak performance, it has strength, vigor, might, and great ability to act. And this is the very definition of power.

Power: "Great or marked ability to do or act; strength; might; force. *C. 1250-1300; Middle English pouer(e), poer(e) < Anglo-French. Poueir, poer, noun use of infinitive: to be able.*"[1]

Like integrity, power is not inherently good or bad. It is not moral. It is agnostic. It is ability. Power can be applied to doing good or doing evil, and more power means more ability to accomplish things. Less power means less ability to accomplish things.

---

1   Dictionary.com. *Dictionary.com Unabridged*. Random House, Inc. http://www.dictionary.com/browse/power,(accessed: April 28, 2017).

The people of a peak performance culture can dare and accomplish noble and mighty things, because they have mastery over the generation of power. And just as integrity is the root of trust, alignment is the root of power, and alignment is generated and maintained through *conversations.*

> *Conversation generates alignment, generates power, generates ability.*

A racecar may be composed of great parts that have the potential to create a powerful driving experience, but if the front end is out of alignment and the timing is off, that potential power will never be realized. The same is true with your organization. It may be made up of great people, but, if they are not aligned, they will never be able to fully generate power.

There are four conversations that the people in your organization can have that will generate alignment and that will consequently have an immediate impact on your power and your ability to get things accomplished:

THE FOUR ESSENTIAL CONVERSATIONS OF ALIGNMENT FOR POWER GENERATION

1. Conversation to Generate Alignment on Perspective: These are conversations to establish a shared perspective on how the organization works and how its parts are interconnected and interdependent. Questions include:

    a)   How do people, money, deals, and products
          or services flow in and out of our system?

b) How do these flows interrelate, and what are their interdependencies?

c) What controls the rate of these flows?

d) Where are the delays in needing something and having it?

This conversation is usually supported by the development of one or more models.[2] Think of this as getting a shared perspective on the underlying physics of the organization.

2. Conversations to Generate Alignment on Intent: These are conversations to establish a broadly felt creative tension between the current state of the organization and its desired future state—making clear what is at stake if things remain as is and making clear what actions need to be taken. Questions include:

a) What is the current state of our organization? (Note: Moral courage is required.)

b) What are the trends and dynamics in our marketplace that we cannot control but are certain to affect us?

c) What are the consequences and implications if we simply keep doing what we are doing the way we are currently doing it?

d) What are we striving for? What is our ennobling vision for our marketplace, our customers, and for ourselves? (Note: The order is important. See: Discipline Three.)

e) What are the fewest, most important things we can commit to doing to progress toward realizing our vision, and how will we guard ourselves from the trap of doing only a little about too many things?

---

2   See the appendix for an example of a model demonstrating the use of conversation to generate a shared perspective in a professional-services organization.

3. Conversations to Generate Alignment on Actions: Informed by 2-e above, these are conversations to establish agreement on what, specifically, will be done by whom and when. Questions include:

a) What specific outcome do we want to have within the next three to six months? (Note: Regardless of how mighty the vision (2-d above), your odds of achieving it go up if you pursue it by stringing projects together, each of which should have a specific outcome and take six months or less to complete.)

b) What resources will we allocate, including people, money, and things, to accomplish these outcomes?

c) What decision authority are we giving the people we ask to achieve these outcomes?

d) What can the people generating these outcomes expect from the rest of the organization as far as access and assistance are concerned?

e) How should we communicate this to the organization in a manner that minimizes resistance, fear, and risk, and promotes collective commitment to success?

f) What are the rewards of success and the consequences of failure?

4. Conversations to Generate Alignment on Culture: These are conversations that generate agreement on the behaviors that are tolerated and advocated for, and the behaviors that are not tolerated. Questions include:

a) What behaviors are we currently tolerating and advocating for, and what behaviors are we intolerant of? (Note: Moral courage required. This is a truth-telling conversation, which means describing things as they actually are.)

    b)   What are the consequences of choosing to continue with our existing culture?

    c)   What new commitments can we choose to make with integrity regarding the behaviors we tolerate and the ones we do not?

    d)   How will we handle breaches of these commitments?

With all these conversations going on, you might be wondering, "So when are we going to stop talking and start getting things done?"

The good news is that you are already having all these conversations in some way or another, or you would not be in business. The only difference is that, in a peak performance culture, there is an intentionality regarding these conversations, and there is mastery in the frequency and manner in which these conversations are conducted. In a peak performance culture, people are always sensing the degree of alignment that others have around these topics, and they are on guard to keep the power-destroying force of fragmentation at bay.

On the opposite end of the scale:

Fragmentation erodes power, erodes ability

Like rust, the forces of fragmentation never sleep. Fragmentation does not need to be generated. Nature only has three laws, and the second one is that systems go from order to chaos, unless an effort is made to maintain order. A peak performance organization does not "have" alignment. Instead, it continuously generates it, because, as power-producing as alignment is, it is an unnatural state.

SHAPE YOUR CULTURE

ANSWER THE FOLLOWING QUESTIONS ON YOUR OWN:

Can you state the mission, vision, and strategy of your organization?

To what extent do your organization's mission, vision, and strategy determine what you do and the decisions you make daily?

ANSWER THE FOLLOWING QUESTIONS AS A GROUP:

Who are the fewest, most important people in your organization who must be aligned to keep your organization focused and powerful?

To what degree are the people in your organization operating from a shared perspective (model) of how the parts of your organization are interconnected and interdependent?

To what degree are the people in your organization aligned around the following:

1) *The description of the organization as it is, not as they want it to be.*

2) *How the organization occurs to its customers.*

3) *The environmental dynamics that are affecting the future of the organization.*

4) *The urgency of change.*

5) *The vision for the organization's future.*

6) *The fewest, most essential actions that your organization must take to continue to thrive.*

MORAL COURAGE

STANDING ON PRINCIPLE, IN DANGER, FOR AS LONG AS IT TAKES

Although I've noted the importance of some disciplines over others, such as the customer, each one is individually valuable, and they are all substantially more valuable when seen as a system of disciplines that complement each other. They have, if you will, interconnectedness and interdependencies. I say this because the seventh and final discipline is one of the most powerful, and yet it's the least understood, and, judging by the news, perhaps in shortest supply. I am talking about moral courage.

As with all seven of the disciplines to practice, our history is steeped with examples of morally courageous people: Gandhi, King, Luther, Socrates, Bonhoeffer, Tubman, Pankhurst, Joan of Arc, Lincoln, Scholl, and Niemöller, just to name a few. These people chose to step into known danger, driven by principle, and endure that danger until they achieved their goal—even if it never occurred.

MORAL COURAGE

- Choosing freely to step into known danger
- Driven by and standing for a principle
- Willingness to endure that danger until the goal is achieved, if at all

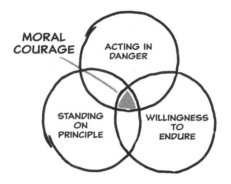

I must give all the credit to the late Dr. Rushworth Kidder, founder of the Institute for Global Ethics, for both helping me see this distinction and then helping me to see how critical it is in generating a peak performance culture. Dr. Kidder said to me that it was not so much a financial crisis that ushered in the new century, but a crisis in moral courage. Take Enron, the NASA *Challenger*, Chernobyl, and Wells Fargo. In every case, enough people had enough information to know that there was potential for a catastrophe, and yet they did not have sufficient moral courage. They existed in cultures that did not nurture and generate it, and that led to tragedy.

If you choose to be the cause in generating a peak performance culture in your organization—and I so hope you do—know that you are putting yourself in danger. Some people do not like to change, and the ones benefiting from some of the behaviors that are accepted now are going to feel threatened by your stand. Many will embrace you and stand with you, but resistance is guaranteed and often becomes hurtful. Welcome to the club of the morally courageous.

Moral courage, or the lack thereof, is easy to see and experience. The next time you gather with others in your organization to discuss a matter of substance, know that a perimeter fence will be established quickly. Inside that fence are the things that the group is willing to say out loud. Outside the fence are the things they know about but are not willing to say out loud. The people of a peak performance culture are continually generating the largest perimeter fence by both making it less dangerous for people to share difficult but vital things and by letting people know that they are expected to do what they feel is right despite the danger they feel.

PERIMETER

Peak performance cannot be realized if critical information contained in the system is not made known to people with the necessary authority to act on it.

SHAPE YOUR **CULTURE**

ANSWER THE FOLLOWING QUESTIONS ON YOUR OWN:

How easy do others make it for you to tell the truth?

How good are you at making it easy for others to tell you the truth? How do you know it's working?

What principles do you refuse to compromise?

Do you feel valued by your organization when you take principle stands?

ANSWER THE FOLLOWING QUESTIONS AS A GROUP:

How much value does your organization place on truth-telling?

How easy does your organization as a whole make it to tell difficult yet valuable truths?

What principles does your organization refuse to compromise? What does your organization do to make these core principles known?

How does your organization let people know what is expected of them when they see these core principles being compromised?

How are truth-tellers dealt with?

Why do you think "moral courage" has been included as one of the seven disciplines to practice of a peak performance culture?

T his book was written for those who refuse to take things as they are and who believe that they can be the cause of something better. I want you to know that you're not alone—that there is a whole community of change agents out there who wake up believing that they can make a difference; that they can be the cause of a better culture.

And that's the truth. That's why my company, The Clearing, exists. We can look at any given situation and change the experience. We don't look at things and say, "Why?" as in, "Why is this happening?" We look at things and say, "Why not?" as in, "We can make a difference and we can do it starting immediately."

Whether you read all of Carolyn's story or dove straight into the "Strike a Match" field guide, I am honored and grateful that you willingly invested time in this book, and I hope it has encouraged you to change the tide at your workplace and to strike your own match to spark a peak performance culture.

I want to close this book with both a prediction and a warning. As you strike your match and take your stand to create a peak performance culture, you and those you enroll will encounter four kinds of people:

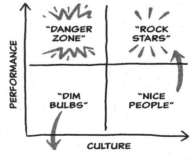

FOUR QUADRANTS

In quadrant #1 you will find people who are not that good at performing and not that aligned with the disciplines and ways of being of a peak performance culture. They should be moved out of the organization.

In quadrant #2 you will find people who are deeply aligned with the disciplines and ways of being of a peak performance culture, but are marginal producers. Invest in these folks to increase their performance; find a place where they can perform at a high level, or, if that fails, move them out.

In quadrant #3 are your high producers who also stand strongly for the disciplines and ways of being of a peak performance culture. Give these people whatever they need. Your future depends on them.

It is in quadrant #4 where your moral courage will be tested. This is where you find high producers who are acting at cross purposes to the disciplines and ways of being of a peak per-formance culture. Examples of mishandling these folks abound. Their retention is rationalized, and excuses are made for them in so many ways, but the fact is that they should be fired. If they aren't, their behavior becomes the default culture, no matter what you say or do. If their behavior is tolerated, then they alone will define the culture of the organization. Fire them. Others will step up. Trust me.

Good luck. Strike that match!

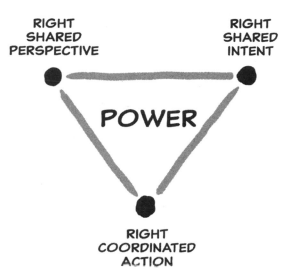

RIGHT
SHARED
PERSPECTIVE

RIGHT
SHARED
INTENT

POWER

RIGHT
COORDINATED
ACTION

Example of a model used to support a conversation to generate shared perspective of how a professional-services organization works.

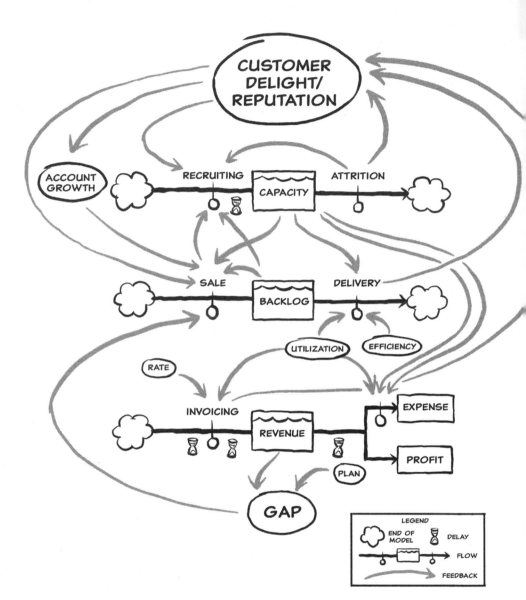

MODEL OF A
PROFESSIONAL-SERVICES
ORGANIZATION

USING MODELS TO GALVANIZE SHARED PERSPECTIVE

Peak performance cultures generate enormous power though the alignment of all key people around:

- The right shared perspective
- The right shared intent
- The right coordinated actions

The right shared perspective means that all the key people in the organization have a common answer to the following key questions:

1) What business are we in?

2) What flows through our company? What controls the rate of flow and where do things accumulate?

3) How are things connected, interrelated, and interdependent?

4) Where are the constraints to performance?

5) Where are the delays in the system that must be eliminated or managed?

6) Where are the levers of growth?

Without a shared perspective to the answers to these questions among all the key people the organization will not achieve full power to achieve its intent. Deep alignment generates full power. Fragmentation erodes power quickly. People become busy but not effective. Duplication and redundancy flourish. People start doing a few things about everything instead of everything about the fewest most important things.

Explicit models are the most effective way to generate shared perspective and alignment around answers to these essential questions. The good news is that there are only 5 types of businesses thus only 5 models and they are all already designed and available for general use. The five types of businesses are:

1) **Service**—Sells time by the hour or deliverable measured by number of billing people at a utilization at al rate.

2) **Product**—Sells things at cost per unit or copy measured by price sold compared to cost to make.

3) **Channel**—Operates connection between makers and consumers measured by percentage of revenue retained.

4) **Operation**—Sells capability to complete tasks measured by per unit processed.

5) **Exchange**—Operates connection between many makers and many buyers measured by subscription fees or transaction fees.

By way of example I have included a system dynamics model of a services firm. Think of it as representing the physics of any business that sells time, whether a doctor's office, law firm, consulting company, accounting firm, or architectural firm. The model makes clear:

1) Invoices, thus revenue, is a function of capacity being utilized at a given rate.

2) People (capacity), backlog (work on contract not yet delivered) and money are the three elements that flow in the system.

3) Backlog increases due to sales. Backlog decreases as a result of capacity being utilized at a given efficiency.

4) Amount of capacity must be inextricably linked to and a derivative of sales and delivery.

5) The most powerful growth lever is a delighted existing customer.

6) The most powerful profit lever is to maximize rate.

7) Delays in acquiring capacity, invoicing, and/or getting invoices paid wreaks havoc on the entire system.

8) The easiest way to deal with a surge in backlog is through increase in utilization of existing staff as acquiring new capacity and increasing the efficiency of existing capacity all have delays from when you ask for it until you get it. Increase in utilization is immediate and drives immediate revenues and profit.

This model has been used extensively to galvanize shared perspective among key people in hundreds of service companies. It is dependable in making 'over there' disappear and making clear the inter-relationships and interdependencies of the various parts of a services business. Models for the other 4 types of businesses are available upon request.

Dear Reader,

I founded my company, The Clearing, to help organizations like Phossium and, very possibly, like yours. When organizations are faced with a changing landscape, when their growth has slowed and they find that their teams are no longer functioning at their best levels, and their systems have become far too complex, then The Clearing is here to help.

We are a management consulting firm that inspires and outfits team members and leaders with the tools they need to make extraordinary contributions to their organization. We eliminate the clutter, innovate, solve complex problems, and transform organizations so that they can better serve their customers and stakeholders; because ultimately, the soul of any successful organization is the customer.

I hope that this book has moved you to take a closer look at your own organization's culture, and inspired you to do what's necessary to ensure that it is a powerful driver of peak performance. And if you need help getting there, we're here.

To learn more about The Clearing,

visit our website **www.TheClearing.com**,

email **info@theclearing.com**,

or call **202.558.6499**.

—Chris McGoff